Politics and Fate

THEMES FOR THE 21ST CENTURY

Titles in this series

Zygmunt Bauman, *Globalization: The Human Consequences*
Zygmunt Bauman, *Community: Seeking Safety
in an Insecure World*
Norberto Bobbio, *Left and Right: The Significance of a
Political Distinction*
Alex Callinicos, *Equality*
Diane Coyle, *Governing the World Economy*
Andrew Gamble, *Politics and Fate*
James Mayall, *World Politics: Progress and its Limits*
Ray Pahl, *On Friendship*

Politics and Fate

ANDREW GAMBLE

Polity

First published in 2000 by Polity Press in association with Blackwell Publishers Ltd

Editorial office:
Polity Press
65 Bridge Street
Cambridge CB2 1UR, UK

Marketing and production:
Blackwell Publishers Ltd
108 Cowley Road
Oxford OX4 1JF, UK

Published in the USA by
Blackwell Publishers Inc.
Commerce Place
350 Main Street
Malden, MA 02148, USA

Library of Congress Cataloging-in-Publication Data
Gamble, Andrew.
  Politics and fate / Andrew Gamble.
    p. cm.—(Themes for the 21st century)
  Includes bibliographical references and index.
    ISBN 0-7456-2167-8—ISBN 0-7456-2168-6 (pbk.)
  1. Political science. 2. Authority. 3. State, The. 4. Fate and fatalism. I. Title. II. Series.
JA71.G25 2000
320—dc21

                                                                    00-033613

Typeset in 10.5 on 12 pt Plantin
by SetSystems Ltd, Saffron Walden, Essex
Printed in Great Britain by T. J. International, Padstow, Cornwall

This book is printed on acid-free paper.

For Chris
a simple twist of fate

Real history is heavy with fate but free of laws.

Oswald Spengler

Few men seem to realise how many of the evils from which we suffer are wholly unnecessary, and that they could be abolished by a united effort within a few years. If a majority in every civilised country so desired, we could, within twenty years, abolish all abject poverty, quite half the illness in the world, the whole economic slavery which binds down nine tenths of our population; we could fill the world with beauty and joy, and secure the reign of universal peace. It is only because men are apathetic that this is not achieved, only because imagination is sluggish, and what always has been is regarded as what always must be. With goodwill, generosity, intelligence, these things could be brought about.

Bertrand Russell

A world in which the possibility of war is utterly eliminated, a completely pacified globe, would be a world without the distinction of friend and enemy and hence a world without politics.

Carl Schmitt

Politics represents at least some tolerance of differing truths, some recognition that government is possible, indeed best conducted, amid the open canvassing of rival interests. Politics are the public actions of free men.

Bernard Crick

Made weak by time and fate, but strong in will.

Tennyson

Contents

Preface   ix

1 Fate   1
2 The End of History   19
3 The End of the Nation-State   38
4 The End of Authority   57
5 The End of the Public Domain   77
6 Politics   96

   Bibliography   121
   Index   125

Preface

This book explores the current disenchantment with politics in the West. Politics was once regarded as an activity which could give human societies control over their fate. There is now a deep pessimism about the ability of human beings to control anything very much, least of all through politics. This new fatalism about the human condition claims we are living through a major watershed in human affairs. It reflects the disillusion of political hopes in liberal and socialist utopias in the twentieth century and a widespread disenchantment with the grand narratives of the Enlightenment about reason and progress, and with modernity itself. Its most characteristic expression is the endless discourses on endism – the end of history, the end of ideology, the end of the nation-state, the end of authority, the end of the public domain, the end of politics itself – all have been proclaimed in recent years. Our contemporary fate is to live in the iron cages erected by vast impersonal forces arising from globalization and technology, a society which is both anti-political and unpolitical, a society without hope or the means either to imagine or promote an alternative future. I argue against the fatalism implicit in so many of these discourses, as well as against the fatalism that has always been present in many of the central discourses of modernity, and set out a defence of politics and the political, which explains why we cannot do without politics, and probes the complex relationship between politics and fate, and the continuing and necessary tension between them.

As it is in the form of an essay, I have dispensed with footnotes and sources so as not to clutter the text and interrupt the flow of the argument. A few authors are named where not to do so would be misleading, but my aim is not to provide an exposition of particular thinkers but to explore some of the general themes which are to be found in contemporary western writing on politics. I have provided a list of references at the end to indicate the kind of sources to which readers can turn if they wish to read further on some of the issues raised in the book.

One of the inspirations for this book was *In Defence of Politics* written by Bernard Crick, once Professor of Politics at Sheffield. It was one of the first books on politics I ever read, and although my argument and my understanding of politics is different from his, it stems from a similar appreciation of the importance of politics as an activity, and the need to defend it.

The Political Economy Research Centre has provided a very stimulating environment in which to think about the themes discussed in this book. I would like to thank all those associated with PERC over the last few years for their intellectual support and encouragement, but I owe special debts to Gavin Kelly, David Marquand, Ankie Hoogvelt, Jonathan Perraton, Michael Kenny and Tony Payne. The last two both read an earlier draft of the book and offered many helpful suggestions and criticisms, as did a reader for Polity Press. I fear I have failed to do justice to them all. I would also like to thank Duncan Kelly, Matthew Festenstein, James Meadowcroft, Carey Oppenheim, Nick Stevenson, Claire Annesley, Steve Ludlam, Tony Wright, Ben Clift, Ian Kearns, Daniel Drache,

Bruce Pilbeam, Alexandre Guimaraes, Teruhisa Tse, Rajiv Prabhakar and Justin Bentham for many ideas and rewarding discussions.

I am also grateful to David Held, Gill Motley and Lynn Dunlop at Polity for their encouragement and patience throughout the writing of this book, and to Tom, Corinna and Sarah for not being too critical.

Andrew Gamble
Sheffield

1

Fate

If politics were at an end, if this was our fate, what would this mean for us? In the modern era politics has promised to give human societies control over their fate, by creating a space, a political realm, in which to seek answers to the fundamental questions of politics – who we are, what we should get, how we should live. Politics understood in this way involves identity and allegiance, power and resources, order and rules. It signals the constant clash of interests, ideologies and values, generating rival parties and movements, alternative principles of social and economic order, and competition to realize them. It is about the formation of public will and public purpose, the determination of the public interest, what should be conserved and what reformed, what should be public and what private, and the rules by which societies should be governed. Underpinning all these notions, however, is the belief that what becomes of us and our societies is in our own hands.

Events in the twentieth century dented this optimism, and spread scepticism about the ability of human beings any longer to control anything very much, least of all through politics. Alternative views of politics as an activity have become prevalent. The first scorns politics as irretrievably conservative, riddled with corruption, waste,

inefficiency and self-interest, a constant block to innovation and change and the least dynamic part of society.
The other fears it as incipiently totalitarian, exacerbating
conflict, fanning ideological commitment and encouraging
a hubris about human abilities to shape their world that
leads to vicious dictatorships.

Such anti-political sentiments have received a boost
from the outbreak of 'endism'. In recent years there has
been an increasingly apocalyptic tone to much writing on
politics and the media has been awash with books and
articles proclaiming the end of just about everything, but
particularly ideology, history, authority and the nation-
state. All the attributes which once defined politics and
the political realm are declared finished, exhausted, super-
seded. Some proponents of endism bemoan these
changes, but many exult in them. They look forward to
the end of politics itself.

A persistent theme in western thought has been the
dream of a world without politics and without conflict. Is
it possible to realize such a society, or is the political an
irreplaceable aspect of what it is to be human? Many of
the utopias which have infested the western imagination
are indeed unpolitical places; all the tasks which were
previously performed by politics are programmed by an
invisible hand or by a supreme intelligence and require no
further attention. But many of these utopias were envis-
aged as an outcome of politics, after which politics could
be dispensed with. Today it has become commonplace to
assert that politics is withering away, and this before any
utopia, whether libertarian or collectivist, has been
achieved. The present age has been declared anti-political
and unpolitical; there is an urge to discredit and disparage
politics, and as faith in politics declines, so concern with
politics and involvement in politics decreases. The space
for politics is shrinking, and with it the possibility to

imagine or to realize any serious alternative to our present condition. This it seems is our fate.

The Idea of the Political

It need not be. Politics still has much to offer. But the meaning of politics and the political are currently rather poorly understood, partly because they do not have a single uncontested meaning. Politics is often used descriptively to refer to any aspect of government affairs and political life in general as well as to the science and art of government, which makes it an omnibus term. But it has also been used in more precise ways. These depend upon defining what is the nature of the political, and how it is to be distinguished from other ways of seeing the world. One of the characteristic features of political thinking is that its codes are binary – it employs fundamental oppositions between the public and the private, between friends and enemies, between the included and the excluded. These oppositions give rise to three distinct and at times rival conceptions of the political.

The major divide is between those who see politics as the activity within a settled polity that creates a public domain and a public discourse through which competing interests are conciliated and society governed, and those who see politics as the activity which first constitutes and then maintains the state as a sovereign political entity by identifying who belongs to it and who does not. The first is built upon the distinction between the public and the private, and the second on the distinction between friends and enemies. In the former the political only comes into existence if there is a public domain – a set of institutions which recognize diversity and allow space for deliberation, negotiation, the representation of interests and the expression of identities. Government is part of this public domain but not the whole of it, and is contrasted with politics. Government can exist while politics is suppressed, either because there are no channels through which the interests and opinions of civil society can be articulated as in authoritarian regimes, or because, even although they are articulated, the actual practice of government is insulated from them, as in some democracies.

For the second conception of the political, however, the determination of what is public and private through forms of deliberation and representation has much less significance than the determination of identity, the basis of every political entity. The state is regarded as the supreme association to which individuals belong, not just one among many, because ultimately it can require the sacrifice of the lives of its citizens in war, on behalf of the collective body, the nation. As in the first conception, the political depends upon the existence of diversity, but it is not the diversity of interest, opinion and identity within the state that is important, but the diversity which arises from the existence of many states, of many separate exclusive sovereignties, which potentially threaten each others' existence. The state only exists as a *political* entity to the extent that this is true. If a universal state ever came into existence it would therefore not be a political entity, because there would be no *other* against which it could define itself.

Protagonists of these conceptions of the political often label the rival conception as anti-political. The argument is an old one which haunts the western tradition of political thought on the requirements of political order. But the disagreement is perhaps overdone. Both conceptions stress the importance of the political in understanding the modern state, and a full account of the political needs to incorporate both conceptions. The genuinely anti-political theories of our time treat the political not as something central to modern experience but as something which is parasitical upon deeper and more fundamental forces, and can therefore easily wither away. These anti-political arguments are to be found in much of the writing on endism. They claim that in both senses of politics as an activity, the political is waning. The public domain is shrinking and sovereignty is weakening, as technical administration expands and conflicts between states recede.

The third conception of the political is closer to the everyday sense in which the term politics is used. Here, to be political is to take a side, to be partisan. It ties politics to factions fighting for advantage, struggles for power and the advancement of individuals or groups who use principles and values as means to serve their interests but lack deeper attachment to them. Politics is all about manoeuvres, intrigues, conspiracies, cabals, lobbies, manipulation. For this reason it has often been regarded by authority as a destructive and divisive activity, associated with opposition. Politics is what those excluded from power engaged in: 'Confound their politicks; frustrate their knavish tricks . . . God Save the King', as the eighteenth-century British national anthem put it. But repressing this kind of politics has never been easy, and no regime is ever without it. It cannot be kept outside the tent. Its focus is on who has influence, who can set the agenda and who can obtain the decisions which favour their interests. It is the politics of position and place, the politics of patrons and clients, the politics of the court which always grows up around power.

Power, Identity and Order

Politics in this sense will never disappear, and no one really suggests it will. But is it possible that politics could so shrink until eventually only this meaning of the political was left? Are the notions of the political as the creation of sovereignty or a public domain, which have been at the heart of the modern conviction that human societies can shape their future, vanishing from our world? This book argues that they are not and will not. The political realm which is constituted by the three dimensions of the political – politics as power, politics as identity and politics as order – remains a crucial component of human experience and human capacity. A state – to be a state – needs all three. Politics as an activity sustains this realm, and to do so it must engage with all three dimensions of the political, but the actual substance of the political realm is not predetermined in any state. It has to be formed through the activity of politics itself.

Power is the instrumental dimension of the political, which asks the question who gets what, when and how? It is the space in which decisions are made as to who is to be included, and who excluded, who's 'in' and who's 'out'. It determines the way in which resources are allocated, ranging from the distribution of public appointments to the distribution of taxes and benefits, as well as administrative and regulatory decisions which are controlled directly by officeholders. It therefore includes court politics, which is inseparable from every institutionalized system of power, but it is also broader than this, covering the organization of political parties and pressure groups, and the networks and policy communities which have grown up around the extended state. It is concerned with the tasks of seeking common ground, building consensus and coalitions, bringing adversaries together, finding solutions which command sufficient consent and legitimacy, gaining access to decision-makers. The role of politicians as brokers between the diverse interests which make up the polity is a crucial one in a democratic system, and conspicuous by its absence in an authoritarian system. But all systems need some mechanism for allocating public offices, public contracts, taxes and benefits. As such, it retains its perennial fascination, not least because of the enormous variations between different cultures and political systems.

Identity is the expressive dimension of the political, which asks the question 'who are we?'. It is the space where choices have to be made between values and principles, where people define who they are, where they embrace or acknowledge an identity, and take on a particular set of commitments, loyalties, duties and obligations. Choosing or affirming an identity means seeing the world in particular ways, and such identities are necessarily defined in relation to other identities. Politics is here about understanding the world in terms of us and them, of friends and enemies. Political identities can be relatively unchanging, or they can be much more fluid, determined as they are by the contingencies of age, gender, class, nationality, religion, ideology and ethnicity. They can be relatively one-dimensional, or they can be complex and overlapping. The most significant identity of all is the state itself, because this creates the basis for other forms of politics. If everyone shared the same values, different political identities would not exist, but so long as experience is diverse, so will values be, and the space is created for the construction, elaboration and adaptation of many different identities which have political relevance. This space is a political space, and political parties may seek to colonize it and control it, but they cannot monopolize it.

Much of the energy and emotional charge of politics comes from the unpredictable deep currents which determine political identities, a world away from the self-interested manoeuvrings of metropolitan elites.

Order is the regulative dimension of the political, which asks the question 'how should we live?'. It is the space which determines the framework of all social activities, the creation and enforcement of binding rules. This includes what is understood as the constitution of the state, the rules determining the powers of the different branches of government, mechanisms of representation and election, rights and responsibilities, but it is also much broader. What is also constitutive of a polity and a society are the institutional arrangements which shape the patterns of social exchange and interaction within that society. These are the institutions of governance which are wider than government itself, and include such things as markets, networks and households, as well as communities and associations. All such modes of governance of a society and economy have ultimately to receive political sanction and be politically sustained. Many of these institutions may not be the subject of any political disagreement and may appear therefore as emanations of nature. But in any social crisis, the ultimate political foundation of social order is revealed.

These three dimensions of politics – power, identity and order – all involve conflict: conflict over who takes decisions as to how resources are allocated, and what those decisions are; conflict over identities of many different kinds and how these are expressed and represented; conflict over the constitutive principles of different political, economic and social orders. Out of them arises a distinctive, multilayered conception of the political, which believes in the contribution politics can make both to ordering and to changing the world. It is this conception which is being challenged by the contemporary resurgence of fatalism.

The Idea of Fate

Human beings have always been obsessed with fate. It hangs over them like a dark shadow. Fate implies finitude; the knowledge that life, whether of the individual or of the species, has natural limits. The fate of each person is their death, and the fate of the species is the extinction of life on the planet whether because of the finite span of existence of the sun, or some other natural cause. Fate in this sense has always been an important component of human culture, deriving its power as an idea from the fact that there are features of the human condition which are inevitable and unalterable. Life stands in opposition to it in a permanent creative tension.

Fate also implies destiny. Once these natural limits are understood they define our destiny. But fate can mean destiny in another sense also, the idea that we are predestined in very particular ways; not just because every life must end, but because every life has a predetermined pattern and content. The particular events which constitute that life and the particular circumstances which end it are all preordained; they have somehow been determined in advance, rendering any notion of free will or choice irrelevant. Our fate is something which exists outside ourselves, and which once revealed expresses the meaning of our lives. Apart, however, from soothsayers who claim to have a means of foretelling exactly what will befall us, this kind of fate is only normally revealed after a life has ended. Only then can the meaning of that life be understood.

Our notions of fate are therefore bound up with our

notions of end, which can signify termination, extinction, death – as, most obviously, the end of life. But it can also be used to signify the meaning or purpose of a human life. Both notions of end have been applied to understand social change and development. At the end of the twentieth century an avalanche of books and articles proclaiming the end of history, the end of the nation-state, the end of politics all but buried the more reassuring announcements of the end of the world. Such writing seeks to reveal the fate of the modern world and modern civilization. But apart from a few prophets who believe that the last days really are (finally) upon us, the proponents of endism do not believe that modern societies are about to become extinct. Rather what they claim is that certain old ways of understanding the world, certain old patterns of behaviour and certain kinds of institution are at an end, and that new ones are preparing to take their place, or are already here.

Claims that we are witnessing the end of history or the end of politics are arresting but largely rhetorical. Taken literally, endism would imply that certain social forms such as the nation-state have become extinct. Particular dynasties or empires or regimes may fall, but societies and social forms do not end decisively and finally in that sense. The capture of Constantinople by the Turks in 1453 brought an end to the Byzantine Empire and its distinctive civilization which had existed for more than a thousand years. But outside the history of wars and conquests there are few events with such finality. Nor did the end of the Byzantine Empire mean the end of empires. The Ottoman Empire arose in its place. Even revolutions which are supposed to signify a radical historical rupture with the past usually on closer examination are found to have strong elements of continuity with the society and state which existed before the revolution.

The reason for this is not hard to seek. While it is possible to conceive of the extinction of a particular form of state – like the nation-states which have been such a dominant feature of the international system in the last three hundred years, or like the great colonial empires which have now vanished – it is hardly possible to contemplate the extinction of the state itself, still less of entities such as history and politics. To do so would imply the extinction of the civilization and culture of which they are constitutive parts. Even applying the term to particular forms of state like nation-states needs to be used carefully. It would be very surprising if a social form as deeply rooted as the nation-state were suddenly to become universally extinct. At most, it would fade out over a long period.

Use of the term 'end' applied to such entities as nation-states, history or authority is better understood therefore not in terms of extinction but as making a claim that a particular phase of history or politics or mode of authority is in some sense finished; it has been replaced by something else. This change can be understood as a simple substitution of the new for the old, or as a process in which the old passes over into the new, and becomes subsumed within it. This second understanding of change is the more subtle. It suggests that it is only possible to reflect on a way of life or social form and understand it after it has fully developed all the potential within it and no longer represents a creative force. It continues to exist but it belongs to the past.

Fate as Destiny

These two meanings of end help us better understand fate. In its most common usage, as we have seen, fate signifies destiny, what is meant to happen, something which is predetermined and unalterable. This notion of destiny can be applied both to the human condition itself – the knowledge that we will all die – and to the particular events of a human life. Often it has been imbued with supernatural or theological determination, as in many religions. In classical Greek culture, from which the word is derived, it meant literally 'that which is spoken', a sentence of the gods. A sentence can be favourable or unfavourable. But it has become associated almost exclusively with the latter and with the idea of punishment. We talk of events which were fated to happen. As a result, fate as destiny has acquired a sombre association with death, destruction and ruin, and leads to a particular orientation to the world – fatalism. To be fatalistic is to believe that events are unfolding in such a way that no other outcome is possible; it is to be without hope that any change could be brought about by human agency. This does not mean that the outcomes are always necessarily bad. It is possible to be a fatalist and an optimist. In religious ideas of providence, for example, the world is working in a preordained way but the consequences are benign. It is more usual, however, to find fatalism linked to pessimism. This is picked up in ordinary language. The word fate is rarely used to describe something which happens to an individual which is good; it is much more common to find it applied to events and outcomes which are regarded as bad.

Fatalism is one of the principal orientations towards social change in social and political thought, and the writing on endism is only the latest example of it. Earlier instances include the long line of deterministic doctrines about social development. The end of history, the end of the nation-state or the end of politics are presented as the fate of modernity. These particular forms were fated to pass away; there was nothing anyone could do to prevent it. So, for example, the fate of the nation-state is determined by the process of globalization which undermines and marginalizes it. Once globalization emerged, the nation-state was under sentence of death, because its logic is inexorable and permits only one outcome. Without anyone planning it, the nation-state is on the road to becoming extinct.

Endism can therefore be read as a set of discourses about the fate of modernity. The thread which brings together what is a highly disparate literature is that endism seeks to dethrone the narratives of modernity and modernization which first originated as Enlightenment doctrines. These doctrines were a set of meta-narratives about history and society which rejected cyclical theories of change in favour of an idea of progress. They were associated with the hope that societies might be made less cruel and less oppressive, rather than with the idea common in classical times that history churned forever through repetitive cycles with no hope of any general improvement in the conditions of human societies, or the Christian medieval view that there was salvation – but not in this world, only in the next. The revolutionary ideas of the modern era which crystallized in the great narratives of the Enlightenment, such as liberalism and socialism, harnessed science, democracy and capitalism in a heady mix to advance the idea that individuals could collectively improve their situation and create a society which was an advance on anything that had previously existed in terms of the promotion of human welfare and the prevention of human misery.

Endism is part of the much wider disillusion that has occurred with the ideas of the Enlightenment and with modernity itself as the consequences of modernity have unfolded. This is a very modern fatalism which regards the end of politics, the end of history, the end of the nation-state, the end of authority and the end of the public domain as marking the end of the ambition of human beings to become the controllers of their fate. Instead they have been enslaved by the forces which modernity has unleashed into the world. Human beings are trapped in the set of iron cages which define the modern world: bureaucracy, technology and the global market. These iron cages provide a set of constraints which narrow the possibilities for alternative forms of social organization and human flourishing. They represent a shrinking of hope, and the closing of a space for politics; they signify the disenchantment of the world, in which the ability to change that world, either to go back to some lost golden age before the modern era, or to go forward to a new age of freedom, has been lost, and lost irrevocably.

One of the central claims of the writing on endism is that the twentieth century witnessed the end of the idea of the progress. It has been a long slow death, and so entwined is it with our sense of modernity that it still lingers on even now. The charge against the great Enlightenment narratives is that they were based on the hope that things could improve and would improve – hopes, it is argued, which have now proved baseless. Capitalism has not been replaced by socialism; a global market has emerged but no world government; science has led not to emancipation through knowledge but to an increasingly destructive technological domination of the earth; while democracy has been hollowed out so that instead of a space which permits self-development and human flourishing through participation in public affairs, it has become a means for the alternation of cynical, self-serving professional elites.

Fate as Contingency

The fate of modernity from this perspective is a bleak one. If the narratives which provided order and purpose are no longer credible and have to be abandoned, where will meaning come from? Without the possibility of foundations which can furnish rational criteria for understanding the world and acting in it, we would seem to be condemned to a thoroughgoing relativism in our beliefs, in which the only source of validity would be the immediate circumstances in which we found ourselves. But even this space would be tightly constrained by the iron cages which modernity has created. This totalitarian vision of the death of agency and the death of hope was a recurring one throughout the twentieth century as its special horrors unfolded. But the totalitarian and one-dimensional future it foretells need not involve concentration camps and barbed wire, but only the quiet despair of an entirely individualized world in which the possibility of engaging in any kind of collective project or collective self-determination has disappeared.

But before we abandon ourselves to pessimism, there is another alternative. Let us suppose for a moment that the grand narratives really are at end, and that it is no longer possible for us to believe in the way they construct and order our experience. This might be liberating rather than constraining, since these meta-narratives embodied their own fatalism, and the idea that they have all ended is itself a particular meta-narrative which carries its own fatalistic assumptions. So let us take the end of all meta-narratives seriously, including the meta-narrative of the end of meta-narratives. In their place comes at least the possibility of a new openness, flexibility and opportunity.

How might we describe this space? We do have a

language to do so – it is the language of politics. Politics is a realm of contingency, in which fate is determined by chance and contingency rather than by anything that is preordained. Politics cannot dissolve fate, because it is not possible to imagine a world without constraints. But the existence of politics offers a different view of fate, both our own fate and the fate of our societies. Politics can prevent fate from turning into iron cages of constraint, because the idea of politics is fundamentally opposed to fate understood as inevitable destiny. So long as there is politics, fate is not fixed. Much of the writing on endism seeks to disable politics by pretending that everything is already decided and the future in all its essentials is unalterable. But if fate is understood as contingency, it is no longer something preordained which hangs over us waiting to be discovered, but something which is in part constructed by us.

The claim that politics has ended is the claim that politics as an activity and as a practice aimed at constituting, renewing and transforming social order has been drained of all significance. The tightness of the constraints on human action mean that there is only one possible order. What is being claimed is not just that a particular phase of politics, a particular period of world history, a particular era of the world economy has ended, and a new one has commenced; instead, the world has moved to a stage beyond modernity in which politics as it has been understood in the modern era is no longer relevant. This is the claim which this book seeks to explore and dispute.

The death of politics comes in many different forms. Four different claims are examined here: the end of history, the end of the nation-state, the end of authority and the end of the public domain. In these four endings are contained the thesis of the end of modernity and the idea that we are at a momentous crossroads in which nothing will ever be the same again. The ideological and institutional framework which defined the modern era is being left behind and we are embarking on new and uncharted territory.

This book, in contrast, sides with those who believe that for all the novelty of many contemporary developments we still live within the horizon of modernity. What is occurring is less the transcendence of the conditions of modernity than the full development of the tendencies inherent within it. Much of the endism literature only relates to the end of particular phases of modern development rather than to modern development itself. There are few good reasons for thinking that the changes at the end of the twentieth century amounted to a rejection of modernity. On the contrary the very terms in which their criticisms are couched betray all too clearly their origins in the perspectives and theories of modernity.

At the heart of modernity is a fundamental tension between politics and fate, but the two are inextricably bound to one another. It is not possible for politics to overcome fate or for fate to overcome politics. But the balance between them and the way in which the two terms are understood is crucial. If social thought becomes 'fatalistic' (as much of the writing on endism tends to be) it succumbs to the belief that there is very little scope for human agency to change the world. But the contrasting position that there is only politics and no fate would mean a world in which there were no constraints, everything could be imagined, and everything willed. Such a voluntarist view that human beings can achieve whatever they desire suggests they have no fate other than the one they individually choose. But a more sober appreciation of the human condition recognizes the inescapable tension between agency and constraint and therefore between politics and fate.

One of the ways in which this perspective helps us to understand our condition is that it gives priority to contingency and the factors which determine contingency. Fate is understood not as something out there, outside ourselves. It is something very real for each individual and each society, but it is brought about through innumerable contingencies, accidents of genetics, of personal biography and of history, rather than by the working out of iron laws or universal causal sequences. Understood in this way, fate both constrains and enables. It sets the limits but it also provides the opportunities. The taking up of those opportunities is the activity of politics, understood in its full sense.

2

The End of History

The most radical, and most fatalistic, of all the claims that politics is finished is the end of history. The notion sounds preposterous; if history is at end then surely the human species must be as well. The idea of history is central to the modern understanding of peoples, civilizations and cultures. It supplies narratives of the past which make sense of the present and prepare for the future. If there were no longer any history, an essential dimension of modern experience would be lost, a critical resource for constructing identity and thinking about politics. Without history we would be forced to live entirely in the present; there would no longer be any sense of a past and historical time.

The problem with the end of history, however, is that it does mean several different things, and is used in a variety of ways, and often very loosely. These different meanings need to be disentangled to find out exactly what is being said. The first meaning, which is the most sweeping, was succinctly expressed long ago by Henry Ford – 'history is bunk' – and underpins the dominant postmodern narratives of our time. A second meaning, associated in particular with Francis Fukuyama who relaunched the phrase 'the end of history' on an unsuspecting public in 1989, makes the end of history synonymous with the end of

ideology, or more accurately with the end of alternatives
to the dominant ideology, liberalism. A third meaning
treats the end of history as Hegel did: the end of history is
the revealed meaning of history, the nature of our modern
world. Each of these meanings has very different consequences for the way in which we understand politics, and
for what kind of politics is possible.

History and Postmodernity

Postmodernism in its various forms depends upon a radical rejection of the past and of all attempts to use the past
to understand the present. Postmodernists want to sweep
away all grand narratives, all historical constructions of
the past which attempt to provide meaning and direction
to the present. The past continues to exist, but it can be
constructed and deconstructed in a myriad of ways to suit
whatever purposes individuals wish to pursue. To live
authentically you need to liberate yourself from the burden of the past, its memories, its identities and its
constraints.

The chief target of postmodernists, as the term suggests,
is modernity itself. They want to dispute any meta-narrative, any framework of understanding which lays down in
advance how we should interpret our present experience
and orient our actions. This makes postmodernists, in an
irony many acknowledge, into the most relentless modernizers. What they most want to be free of is 'history' in the
sense of those constructions of the past which bind action
and thinking in the present. Chief among such constructions are the great Enlightenment ideologies of the modern era: socialism, liberalism, communism.

What postmodernists object to in these meta-narratives
are the assumptions that history has an objective meaning,

that history can be interpreted as moving towards a definite goal, whether liberty or the classless society, and that the way in which we interpret the past can give us guarantees about the future. Once the objectivity of any picture of the past is denied, history dissolves into a myriad of subjective narratives, none intrinsically more valid than any other, and all relative to time and place.

Postmodernism and postmodernity are in one sense extremely misleading terms, since they suggest that they come after modernism and modernity, when actually they have always been present from the very start. The postmodern attitude is there in Marx's cry: 'the tradition of all the dead generations weighs like a nightmare upon the brain of the living', and it has shaped the mood of generations of modernizers. To be modern means to question and criticize all received knowledge and to welcome change and novelty and innovation. Modernity has involved a particular kind of consciousness which is embodied in progressive ideologies such as liberalism and socialism, but also in fascism and some forms of nationalism.

In their time liberalism and socialism were modernizing and radical, the enemy of traditions and fixed beliefs. But for postmodernism they have now become ossified and an obstacle to future development, rather than an aid to it. The claim of the great ideologies cannot be substantiated or verified. In proclaiming the end of all meta-narratives postmodernists argue that there is no objective basis for a politics either of reform or of reaction. All positions are equally subjective and arbitrary. History offers no guide and no criteria, although some postmodernists deny that this entails the embrace of radical subjectivism and relativism; it is possible to deny that there are foundations for our ideologies or beliefs without feeling the need to abandon those beliefs. We can still choose to hold those beliefs and support a certain kind of regime and social order because they correspond to the values we espouse.

Where postmodernism is most novel is the radicalism of the break it wishes to make with all the ideologies which have hitherto provided us with ways of interpreting modernity and its development. This is presented as the justification of thinking of the present period as a radical disjuncture with the past, a new stage of development, postmodernity. But even describing it in these terms reveals how trapped we remain in the old language – a new stage of development implies earlier stages of development, a radical disjuncture or watershed implies a particular understanding of how the present relates to the past, postmodernity implies that there was once something called modernity. All these assumptions from a thorough-going postmodernist perspective are suspect. This is the reason many people find postmodernist thinking both exhilarating and disorienting – exhilarating because it throws everything up into the air, questions everything, criticizes everything and allows new beginnings and fresh thoughts; but disorienting, because it contains a strong tendency to nihilism. In many earlier manifestations of this aspect of the modern consciousness the tendency to nihilism was held in check by a strong narrative about history and identity. But many variants of postmodernism reject not only all former narratives but all new narratives, since all narratives once they cease to be simple subjective constructions are vulnerable to the charge that they depend on foundations. These foundations may no longer be claims to a knowledge of reality which is objective and universally valid; they more often depend on claims about intersubjective understandings and agreement. Many leading postmodernists will have nothing to do with it. For them it is just another way to smuggle back meaning into the world, and confer importance once more on politics. From this standpoint the postmodern perspective means accepting that politics has become trivial and meaningless, irrelevant to the way we live our lives.

Radical forms of postmodernism therefore end up rejecting history and with it the possibility of politics, because they are reluctant to concede any of the foundations for the narratives which are necessary for politics to succeed. This has not prevented many who are influenced by postmodernism from having a strong impact on modern political thinking and practice. But they have done so by developing their own distinctive narratives, which have necessarily involved an understanding and particular construction of history. As with so many forms of endism, the proclamation of the end of history and the end of ideology and even the end of meta-narratives as far as postmodernism is concerned, does not mean the end of history, ideology and meta-narratives as such, but rather the invention of new forms of all of them.

In this way postmodernism has spawned a new generation of political styles and fashions in western democracies, which seek to reject the past and free themselves from ideological and party traditions, and present themselves as anti–ideological and even anti-political. Modernizing politicians seek to construct a political space in which they can shed what they have inherited from the past and so appear as new and unencumbered. Reinventing themselves is a way to escape from former identities and commitments. But it also makes them rootless and rather indistinct in their beliefs and policies compared to the traditional parties of left and right which defined themselves in relation to particular historical narratives about the past. It also leaves them with the problem of how they can keep reinventing themselves. Permanent revolution and permanent modernization are what is required in the era of postmodernity.

Identity

One of the central objections of postmodernism to the old politics is the relatively fixed and unchanging identities which the major ideologies construct around class, gender, ethnicity, nation and the individual. Postmodernists, in contrast, emphasize difference, fluidity, subjectivity and relativism in understanding how identities are formed; identity, as a result, is contingent, multiple and constantly being negotiated. The meta-narratives of liberalism and socialism, nationalism and ethnicity, and gender claim an objective and immutable basis for their accounts of the social world and of politics. Postmodernist approaches reject the idea that a single identity, for instance class, is capable of defining an individual or of determining the issues with which politics should be concerned. Instead they argue that politics has to be pluralistic to take account of the many and overlapping identities and commitments which individuals have – which include race, gender, class, ethnicity, neighbourhood, locality, nation, work, household, age and sexual orientation.

A key target for postmodernists in their critique of traditional accounts of identity has been the importance ascribed to one particular identity – that based on class – in traditional socialist ideology. Political parties should no longer seek to base themselves on one particular social identity such as the labour movement, believing that this provides a secure and stable foundation. There are no longer any such primary identities which define the political world and the basis of allegiance and belief. Instead, political parties have to assemble a coalition and develop a programme and a style of operation which is sensitive to the multiple and changing identities which voters have. Parties which become one-dimensional in their appeals to class or nation are only likely to mobilize minorities. The inability and unwillingness of many political parties to adjust to this new world of identity politics has been one reason for the association of identity politics with social movements rather than with mass political parties and electoral politics of the traditional kind, and therefore with increasing distance from traditional forms of politics. The response of the new politics has been the development of new techniques such as focus groups which seek to track the shifting moods and concerns of voters in order to shape the programme, image and style of the party. The focus group can be seen as a typical expression of post-modernity, because it is entirely free from any concern with the historical patterns of allegiance and belief which gave parties their identity, and is concerned only with how the image of the party is currently perceived and how it might be altered to be aligned more closely with the response of ordinary voters as revealed in the focus groups.

Many postmodern accounts of politics emphasize difference, the politics of recognition, and attack fundamentalism. This is because, since postmodernism rejects foundations, it should reject any politics which bases itself upon foundations, such as nationalism. But this is too easy a reading. The recurrent strand of nihilism in postmodern thinking means that all political positions can be accounted for as equally valid and equally false; so that it becomes as legitimate a stance to affirm Nazism as to affirm liberalism. These are subjective choices, and cut adrift from history and tradition there are no anchors or signposts. It gives to the political projects of postmodernity a fragile and subjective character. The choice of one direction over another becomes arbitrary. This free-floating character of political commitment and belief is why nothing determinate flows from a postmodern perspective.

It is perfectly compatible with postmodernism to support liberal democracy and the rule of law; but equally, since it absolves human beings from their ties to the past and from historical forms of identity and belonging, it opens the way to much more destructive and nihilistic forms of politics.

Historicism

A different version of the end of history seeks to revive its original Hegelian meaning. Here, there is no attempt to go beyond modernity but to celebrate one particular interpretation of it. The reason Francis Fukuyama chose Hegel's phrase 'the end of history' as the title of his article is that he wanted to draw attention to the waning force of communism and the coming triumph of liberalism. His timing could not have been better. No sooner had he published the article than the Berlin Wall was opened and the final stages of the collapse of communism in Europe began.

Fukuyama attracted great notoriety for his article, and much incredulity. Some of his critics assumed him to be claiming that there would in future be no more significant events in the lives of societies and nations, nothing to dignify the name of history. What he was in fact doing was reviving a style of argument – liberal historicism: the belief that history has an objective meaning and an ultimate purpose and that there are processes propelling history towards that goal. Liberal historicism of this kind had long been out of favour, ever since it was criticized so strongly by Karl Popper in the 1950s. Many of his fiercest critics were indeed liberals who condemned his argument as trivial, tendentious and misleading. Historicism had been an important part of a certain kind of liberal narrative. It had then become associated with Marxism, through Marx's adaptation of Hegel's categories to depict a process of dialectical struggle between classes which would ultimately result in communism. Much later, Alexandre Kojeve had turned Marx on his head and interpreted this dialectical struggle as a struggle between rival ideologies which, instead of resulting in the triumph of communism, resulted in the triumph of liberalism, vindicating Hegel's insight that the ideas of the French Revolution could not be improved upon as far as the conditions of modernity were concerned.

Hegel's original argument tends to get lost in this twentieth-century liberal historicist discourse. Hegel had certainly been the first to argue that history had ended, but he was very precise about it. The event occurred in 1806 at the battle of Jena. Hegel interpreted the triumph of Napoleon's armies over Prussia as the triumph of the ideals of the French Revolution over the *anciens régimes* of Europe. For Hegel, this victory inaugurated the modern era and established the primacy of the ideas which constituted the institutional order of the modern world: individualism, the importance of the private sphere, freedom and equality, and at the level of the state the acknowledgement of the equal worth of every citizen, a politics of universal recognition.

Hegel could interpret this as the end of history because he understood 'end' in its double sense, both as purpose and as termination. By being at an end, history revealed its meaning. The events of the past only deserved the name history if they could be shown to have a meaning, and a meaning not simply for the individual but an objective meaning, which could be disclosed through rational reflection. History could have such a meaning because it could only be understood as a product of mind, developed through the clash of opposing principles and conceptions of social order: the civic consciousness of the classical world, and the theocratic insistence on the individual soul and on subjective inwardness of the medieval world. The full one-sided development of each of these opposing principles made possible the eventual reconciliation of both of them in a higher stage of human society, the democratic egalitarian order of modernity. This higher stage was founded on the recognition of both human individuality and human collectivity in the institutions of modern society; individuals were simultaneously members of three distinct spheres – the family, civil society and the state – in which all aspects of their personality could be expressed.

The human species has existed on earth in its contemporary form for at least 150,000 years, but the notion of history and of historical time, even in the restricted sense of recording events and constructing simple narratives, is much more recent. Written histories are confined to the last 3,000 years, and arose within particular cultures. The notion of history which Hegel develops takes this sense of historical time, which had become part of the ordinary consciousness of European societies, discerning within the pattern of past events a movement towards a final goal. This movement is not, however, for Hegel something which is embodied in social forces, but a process which takes place within the human mind, reflecting on the past and trying to make sense of its underlying pattern. It is this activity of mind endowing the past with meaning and purpose which makes it into history in Hegel's sense. If the past is simply the record of unconnected random events it cannot be history. To become history, all events, even the most inexplicable, have to be interpreted within a framework which shows how they contribute towards progress to the final stage. When that stage is reached history necessarily ends because its meaning has been revealed. This idea that history has a meaning and that this meaning is the progress of human societies towards freedom, equality and solidarity is one of the key ideas associated with the European Enlightenment and as such became one of the central narratives of modernity.

It is history in this special sense which Fukuyama, following Kojeve, declares to be at an end. To the casual observer there might seem to have been rather a lot of history since the battle of Jena, or even since Kojeve first formulated his ideas in the 1930s. But this is to use history in its more common, everyday use, where it refers to events which are accorded some significance in the life of a group or a nation. Hegel's understanding of the end of history is not affected by considerations like these, since what he means by history is the development of human consciousness and capacity through the working out of the conflict between opposing principles. If all fundamental principles were now reconciled in the grand synthesis represented by the French Revolution, there was no basis for any further stage of development, and therefore no basis for history in Hegel's sense.

An end to history, however, does not require an end to conflict. History for Hegel was at an end because he did not choose to speculate on the future. Philosophy could only interpret what was already in the past. Many historicists influenced by Hegel have argued that further stages of development are possible through the rise of new antagonistic principles of development which continue the dialectical process. But there has been disagreement as to whether these conflicts continued 'history', holding out the prospect of the achievement of a higher stage of development and the emergence of new principles, or whether the principles established at the end of history could not be improved upon, so that whatever the struggles and time required to realize these principles, they themselves were not capable of being transcended. They constitute the stage on which the fate of the modern world is played out. From this standpoint the ideological struggles of the last two hundred years, including in particular the titanic struggle between socialism and capitalism, can be interpreted as struggles over how the principles of the modern world can best be implemented rather than as struggles to replace them by new ones. For liberal historicists the principles for ordering the modern world are fixed, and this means that attempts to improve upon them either by going back to earlier stages of historical development or trying to establish an alternative set of principles will end in disaster and ruin. This is the meaning of the last two hundred years. History has ended twice. Once in 1806 and once more in 1989, when the most important attempt of the last hundred years to provide an alternative to these principles collapsed.

This liberal historicist reading of Hegel and of modernity has never been uncontested. Conservatives rejected the liberal and secular principles of the French Revolution and proposed their own narratives of order, authority and tradition, while socialists argued that although the French Revolution might provide formal political rights, it failed completely to provide social rights, because of the protection it gave to unequal property rights. Hegel's original vision was blotted out for a long time by the Marxist appropriation of Hegel's dialectical method to demonstrate that the end of history (or of prehistory, as Marx liked to call it) would only arrive after the abolition of the class basis of society. Communism not liberalism provided the principles for an emancipated social order, with class struggle as its motor. Faced with the claims of Marxism-Leninism to have laid bare the laws of motion of history and the inevitability of socialism, many liberals became anti-historicists, rejecting the claims of any philosophy of history which purported to reveal its objective meaning.

The End of Ideology

Liberal historicism has now, however, made a triumphant comeback. Communism was tried after a fashion in the twentieth century and proved a spectacular failure. What was hailed at the outset as the first workers' state, a progressive alternative to an increasingly exhausted and discredited capitalism, turned into a backward and repressive prison, and became one of the most conservative and inert regimes in the world. The challenge of socialism as a different organizing principle for modern societies petered out, leaving the revived and self-confident capitalist democracies of the West as the undisputed victors. The 'end of history' has been resuscitated in order to celebrate this event. But this was not the end of history as Hegel understood it, but the end of ideology, or, more precisely, the death of socialism, which had been proclaimed much earlier.

When the claims by Daniel Bell and others about the end of ideology and the death of socialism first appeared in the 1950s they became established then as a kind of liberal common sense. The high tide of socialist advance in the countries of North America and Western Europe was declared over, and the fear of communism, although still intense, became fear of the Soviet Union as an external power, replacing fear of internal socialist revolution. The Soviet Union and the rest of the communist bloc became a world apart, a closed empire which posed a security threat, but a diminishing ideological threat. It continued to offer a practical, if deeply flawed and increasingly inferior, alternative to the capitalism of the West, and supported a military and industrial machine which led to a tense security stand-off between the two blocs. Disillusion with communism was seen as one of the reasons for the death of socialism in the West and the domestic consensus which had been forged between left and right. The right accepted the welfare state and the expansion in the scope and scale of the state which this entailed while the left accepted capitalist property rights as the basis of the economy as well as the importance of limits on state power. The programmes of all the mainstream political parties changed to acknowledge these new realities. In this new, managed mixed economy there was no longer any role for ideology, the imagining and counterposing of alternative social and economic institutional arrangements for governing social and economic life.

The ultimate collapse of the Soviet Union was not a surprise. In the 1950s it had briefly appeared to be a significant competitor as an economic system to western capitalism, mainly through prestige projects such as its space programme and the ability of its command economy to maintain high rates of growth. But by the 1970s the deep problems of the economy, and its inability seriously to compete with the West, were apparent. The speed with which the system unravelled in six short years from 1985 to 1991, however, was remarkable; most observers expected it to last for several further decades and few predicted that its demise was so imminent. Various factors can now be seen to have contributed – the reforms initiated by Gorbachev, the intensification of military competition with the United States, and the upheavals in the Eastern European satellites at the end of the 1980s. The drama of the events which saw the toppling of regime after regime until the fall of the Soviet Union itself was so intense that it revived the idea of the death of socialism.

As a living alternative to capitalism in the western

democracies, socialism in the form of the communist system was already dead, and had long been so. But equally, the fate of socialism and communism had become inextricably entwined in the course of the twentieth century. The fall of communism in the Soviet Union was much more than the downfall of a particular state and its empire. It marked the end of a social and political experiment which had failed in its aim to provide a viable alternative to capitalism, but which had nevertheless become one of the most important shapers of the international state system in the twentieth century. What had seemed a fixed and permanent feature of international politics was swept away almost overnight. These dramatic events did more than anything to make endism respectable. No one could dispute that the disappearance of communist regimes in Europe and the ideological division between West and East marked the end of an important phase of world politics. A major historical watershed had occurred.

But in what sense did this represent the end of history? A particular state – the USSR – had come to an end, and with it a particular regime and its state doctrine, Marxism-Leninism. Only, however, if the Marxist version of the end of history were accepted, and only if the USSR was seen as a true socialist state, could its collapse be plausibly presented as the end of history. From a true Hegelian standpoint, the titanic struggle between capitalism and socialism in the twentieth century was not part of history at all, merely the working out of the principles which had already been established as the guiding principles of the modern era. The end of history happened long ago, and the ideological travails of the modern era, however momentous, have never questioned the fundamental principles which underlie it. What Fukuyama means by the end of history is not really therefore the end of history at all, but the end of socialism, the end of a particular phase of ideological contestation in the modern era. This is quite clear from his original article, where he proclaims the triumph of liberal capitalism.

Modernity and History

The phrase 'the end of history' has since taken on a life of its own, used by many journalists as shorthand for a number of simple propositions about the contemporary political and ideological landscape. The ending of communism follows the earlier ideological convergence between socialists and conservatives over the mixed economy and the welfare state. It means that the long detour of the two hundred years following the battle of Jena are at an end. The alternatives to liberalism which have been tried have failed. The end of history and the end of ideology mean that economic and political liberalism have triumphed, viable alternatives to capitalism no longer exist, the final point in humanity's ideological evolution has been achieved and democratic government and free market capitalism are now universal. They are the horizon of possibility. The old differences between left and right are redundant because there is no longer any prospect of improving on the basic principles of the liberal democratic state or of escaping from the capitalist world economy. All forms of autarchy are dissolving and although different models of capitalism are possible, no economy can any longer survive outside the institutional forms and pressures of the global market.

It is a short step to move from this end of history to the end of politics. Not only will politics have to be conducted within narrow parameters in the future (it often has been in the past), but there is no prospect of the parameters changing drastically and no point in challenging them. The sharper ideological conflict which occurred in the 1970s and early 1980s in many western countries is from this point of view an aberration, a last spasm of the old politics. The convergence of so many parties of left and right towards very similar positions on almost all major policy issues since the end of the 1980s is seen as the shape of things to come. Politics is set to become boring and trivial, of no real concern to citizens, who show their contempt for it by declining in ever greater numbers to come out and vote, to join political parties, or even to keep politically informed.

But the fundamental flaw in all these arguments is the conflation between the end of history and the end of ideology. The contest between historically specific ideologies of capitalism and socialism has been one of the main features of the twentieth century. But the fact that this period has ended with the triumph of 'capitalism' does not mean the death of socialism, but only of one historically specific form of socialism, state socialism. In the same way the disappearance of laissez-faire capitalism in the twentieth century did not signal the death of liberalism. Socialism and liberalism are extremely complex ideological traditions which are able to renew themselves and reinvent themselves. There is no real sign that this process is yet exhausted.

Socialism and liberalism have often been competing ideologies, but that should not blind us to the strong links between the two. Socialism has often been considered an outgrowth or development of liberalism, in the sense that it seeks to fulfil the principles of liberalism rather than replace them. The long argument between markets and planning which was the heart of the ideological contestation between capitalism and socialism in the twentieth century concerned means rather than ends. But many liberals advocated planning, just as today many socialists advocate markets. What is common to both liberals and socialists are the basic values of equality and freedom, and the commitment to universalism. Forms of socialism and of liberalism become discredited, and then reinvented or adapted to changing circumstances. New forms are constantly emerging and will continue to emerge. The underlying aspirations of the Enlightenment have not gone away.

Hegel's construction of the term 'history' may be idiosyncratic and restrictive, and there are few adherents today of his particular philosophy of history. But it does focus attention on the nature of modernity – the structures, institutions and principles of the modern world, which are the product of the end of history. Fukuyama offers no reasons why the end of history should be displaced to 1989. To do so he would have to show that there was some new major principle which has been developed in the last two hundred years and which has now been subsumed within a new order at the end of the twentieth century. But he can demonstrate no such thing. All he can point to is the ideological contestation between liberalism and socialism, which he wants to argue has ended in the complete victory of one side and the collapse of the other. He does not present this as a dialectical process in which the initial opposition between contrasting principles is resolved by the achievement of a higher synthesis in which the positive elements of both principles are preserved.

What Fukuyama and before him Daniel Bell have been describing and commenting on is a particular phase in the cycles of ideological conflict over the best way to realize the fundamental principles and values of western civilization in general, and modernity in particular. This does not constitute history in Hegel's sense. The end of history is being used as a code for the end of ideology, and the end of ideology in turn is code for the end of socialism. If the issue they wish to analyse is the dwindling appeal and declining relevance of a particular form of ideology, then that is one thing. But it should not be confused with the end of ideology, and still less with the end of history.

Ideological debate has been a vital aspect of modernity, and if it were really on the wane there would be a question-mark over modernity itself. Ideology has often passed through cycles, and one way of interpreting the current transformation in socialist ideology and socialist parties throughout Europe is as part of a new phase of the cycle. This is not to deny the enormous watershed in modern history which the collapse of the Soviet Union represents, or its significance for politics and for ideological debate. The lines of argument have indeed shifted, but they have shifted for all parties and all ideologies, and the crisis of belief is general, not confined to socialists. Conservatives have been plunged into their own ideological limbo, torn between their enthusiasm for global markets and liberalization on the one hand and their attachment to the nation-state and national cultural traditions on the other. There are important changes taking place in ideological debate. On the left–right, or socialist–liberal, ideological axis, which measures attitudes to the role of the state in the economy, liberal ideas are in the ascendancy, but the importance of this axis is waning compared with the axis organized around nationalism, ethnicity and identity. The end of ideology, however, is nowhere in sight.

3

The End of the Nation-State

One of the main contemporary examples of fatalism about politics is to be found in the writing on globalization. The story goes like this. The era of the nation-state is over. It has become an anachronism and is facing forces which it can no longer control. The state is in retreat. Power is being drained from it and it is rapidly losing its capacity to shape events. Claims such as these have become commonplace in the discourse on globalization which has been gathering strength since the early 1970s. Advocates of globalization have become increasingly bold in their assertions, particularly since the collapse of communism in Europe and the reunification of the world economy. Nothing can withstand the power of the global market, global communications and global culture. The walls around national cultures, national economies and nation-states are crumbling before the battering-rams of the new global order. Old notions of politics, democracy, legitimacy, sovereignty and planning totter before the onslaught. To be globalized, it seems, is now our fate.

This mantra has been preached with ever greater certainty, even if at first glance the world at the beginning of the twenty-first century appears to be based more around nation-states than it has ever been. The break-up in the last fifty years of continental and colonial empires, culminating in the dismemberment of the former USSR, has led to the founding of many new nation-states and the re-establishment of many more. No nation is too small, it seems, to aspire to have its own state. The international system is based upon the recognition of the importance of the nation-state, and non-interference in the affairs of the nation-states which together comprise the United Nations is regarded as a fundamental principle, which is why it has proved so difficult ever to get UN support for breaching it, even in the case of Kosovo in 1999. This familiar world of nations and their states, with their flags and sports teams, their national anthems and national airlines, national cultures and national capitalisms, is what we are told is being hollowed out by the forces of globalization.

The Global Market

What the discourse of globalization seeks to discredit is that what matters in international politics are relations between states. This simple conception is often traced back to the Treaty of Westphalia in 1648 which ended the Thirty Years War and enunciated the doctrine that each state which was recognized as a legitimate state within the international state system had supreme authority within its own territory. The consolidation, on the one hand, of all local, particular and personal sources of authority into a single public power within a defined public space and, on the other, the repudiation of the claims of universal forms of religious and political authority – such as the Church and the Holy Roman Empire – gave expression to the modern idea of the state. Whether the Treaty of Westphalia is as important in this evolution as has been made out is less important than the fact that this change did take place. By the middle of the seventeenth century an international state system had emerged in Europe and gradually spread to the rest of the world.

Many of the states which were recognized as part of this state system were not nation-states, but like the United Kingdom and Austria-Hungary were multinational states, incorporating many different nations and cultures. Many also acquired extensive colonial empires. Only much later was the nationalist doctrine promulgated that only those states which were nation-states had true legitimacy, which carried the implication that every nation not already a state should seek to become one and take its place within the international state system. In the twentieth century there was a pronounced trend for states to become coterminous with nations. But the fundamental principal of an international state system is not the idea of the nation but the idea of the state. The world is divided up into states which claim absolute sovereignty over the territory and population they control and recognize no superior jurisdiction.

In such an international state system the economy is conceived as an international economy made up of separate national economies, which are controlled to a greater or lesser degree by states which claim authority over specific national territories and their population and resources. All flows of goods, people and capital within this international economy have to be sanctioned by political authority and international agreements. In this system states owe their power to their capacity to control their territory and what goes on within it. But the emergence of a global market is said to make nation-states as centres of decision-making redundant, and with them the entire apparatus of representative politics and state capacities which have been built up in the last 350 years. They belong to a different mode of organizing and understanding the connections between human societies, which focuses on security rather than the economy.

Powerful though this way of conceiving the organizing principle of international politics has been, it has come under severe challenge primarily because the idea of territorial sovereignty no longer captures very well the way in which the global market is governed and the role of states within it. This insight is the origin of the globalization thesis. It views states and all other organizations from the standpoint of the global market rather than from the international state system. A global market is one in which the fundamental units are not nation-states and national economies but patterns of production and consumption organized by transnational companies and other agents, operating across national borders and not reliant on any particular national territory or government. Global financial markets and the patterns of international trade shape national economic policies. National governments which ignore or resist the pressures from the markets, as Britain is said to have done in the 1970s, or France in the 1980s or Sweden in the 1990s, by subsidizing employment, protecting uncompetitive industries or spending more than the markets were prepared to support, risk financial crises. If they persist in such policies, they suffer the penalty of deteriorating economic performance, currency depreciation and low investment.

National governments can choose to work with the grain of global markets or resist them. But if they choose the latter, the globalization thesis predicts they will impoverish their people and precipitate either the fall of the government or political repression. The rise of the global market means that governments lose their autonomy and become ciphers for global economic forces, which act as a battering-ram to break down all obstacles to the free play of competition and exchange. Not only is this process inevitable; it is also benign. By undermining nation-states, hitherto the main actors in the international state system and the world economy, it brings nearer the nineteenth-century dream of a global cosmopolitan society which is co-ordinated and managed without the need for politics and governments. Such a society is united around a single set of political, social, economic and ideological principles. There are no political debates, so no alternatives. In this way some of the hyperglobalist accounts of globalization dovetail with the vision of an end to history. The nation-state has outlived its time because it is a repository of those forces which seek to keep alive ideological division and seek to interfere with the optimum allocation of goods and investment, by clinging to outdated notions of sovereignty. Here, politics is seen as obstructive, inert, reactive and reactionary, a dead weight upon the living, creative, flexible forces of the spontaneous cosmopolitan economic order.

The trends towards globalization are not imaginary. Some real and important changes have been taking place in the world economy, which have weakened nation-states and eroded their sovereignty. But many of the more extreme claims of the hyperglobalists are unconvincing. What is wrong with this way of thinking about inter-national politics is that it treats the global market firstly as if it was a novel form of organization which has only just arrived, and secondly as if it was a natural process, entirely unconnected with politics and political decision-making, as well as with other principles of order.

The global market, however, did not begin in 1991 or even 1971. The contrast between an international politics organized through states and an international politics organized through markets is false. The global market of the modern era predates the consolidation of the Euro-pean international state system in the seventeenth century and has existed in uneasy relationship with it. The history of international politics reflects more than one principle of order. Apart from the cosmopolitan order of the global market there is the territorial order of the international state system, and the hegemonic order of the system of transnational governance, forms of rule for the global market which mediate between the world of states and the world of markets.

These are different principles for understanding international politics and the requirements of world order, and there is nothing natural about them. They are political constructions, which reflect complex political choices and dispositions, give rise to particular institutions, and have to be sustained by political means. Thinking of international politics in this way directs attention to the political aspects of our world, and to the complex interplay between contingencies and choices which determine our fate. However strong the trends which globalization has unleashed, it does not cease to be part of the political or to be governed by politics. At most, what is being claimed is that it introduces a different set of political priorities and political constraints. But this is part of a political argument about the nature of our world. It is very far from signalling an end of politics.

The debate on globalization can be read in this way. The critics of globalization seek to preserve a different set of political choices from those which are embodied in the hyperglobalist account, as well as pointing out that even if it was considered desirable to achieve the priorities of the globalizers, it could only be done through the mechanism of nation-states. That is because so many of the governance mechanisms on which the global market relies are organized and sustained by nation-states. Global economic forces and global markets have existed since the emergence of capitalism, but they have always depended on non-market institutions and in particular systems of governance, both state and non-state. Forms of gover-

nance have been changing in response to changes in the
world economy, but the idea that global markets themselves could supply their own internal mechanisms of
governance is naive.

Regionalism

The implications of globalization as a set of economic
trends for policy in any one nation-state are uncertain.
Does membership of regional economic groupings, for
example, help or hinder a state to adjust to globalization?
States in many parts of the world have come under
pressure to participate in some form of regional economic
grouping. It is most developed in Europe, but there is a
lively debate within the European Union as to the desira-
bility of deepening or widening European integration.
Those who oppose widening often do so because they do
not want to dilute the advantages of the existing union; in
particular they oppose labour migration. Those who
oppose deepening often see it as a move towards the
creation of a European super-state. Such a state, they
argue, would run counter to globalization because it
would be centralized, protectionist and bureaucratic,
rather than dynamic, enterprising and responsive to rapidly changing costs and markets in the fastest growing
economies in the world in East Asia and North America.

Supporters of the European Union project believe that
both deepening and widening are desirable objectives, and
that only through the creation of effective supranational
as well as sub-national levels of governance can the kind
of non-market institutions be created to sustain a European economy which enjoys high income and high welfare. They argue that regionalization is necessary to give
states sufficient capacities to influence the impact that

globalization has on their economies. The anti-Europeans ignore the links between regionalization and globalization, which makes their policies in practice protectionist and isolationist. The pooling of national sovereignty is inescapable in a global market because interdependence creates problems which can no longer be solved at the national level.

The argument for regionalist projects in other different parts of the world is similar. It is often political rather than economic. It provides capacities which nation-states can no longer provide, and it increases economic security. There is considerable difficulty in developing such regional groupings outside Europe, however, because of the imbalance that exists between the state or states in the core and those on the periphery. This is most obvious in the Americas because of the position of the United States, but is also true in East Asia, because of the existence of two potential leading states – Japan and China. Outside these three developed regions, in Africa or South Asia, there is very little regional cooperation. But without such political structures and forums the ability of states, particularly in the South, to shape the global market to their own requirements is very limited.

The Neo-Liberal Project

Globalization therefore denotes certain economic trends but also a particular normative ideological project which supports particular policies and rules out alternatives. In this second sense it has been used to justify substantial changes in domestic policies, particularly on public spending, welfare, industrial intervention and prices and incomes policy. Acceptance of the new constraints and the changed balance between national governments and global markets has become the new political wisdom and political orthodoxy.

There is, however, not one globalization discourse but several. Acceptance that there is something called globalization, or at least that there exist certain trends towards a more integrated global market, is not the end of the argument but the beginning of it, since there are so many different ways in which states and groups can adjust to these changes. It is very difficult to imagine what a contemporary political argument would look like which paid no attention at all to globalization, since that would mean paying no attention to the global market, which has been an unavoidable political reality for several centuries. No political doctrine or political programme in any part of the world can easily ignore the global market, the trends within it, and their implications for territorial sovereignty and transnational governance.

Once the discourses of globalization are viewed politically, they become much easier to understand and to assess. The visions found in some popular versions of globalization of a cosmopolitan order beyond politics is revealed as a particular political fantasy, the political conditions for which, although not impossible, would be very hard to guarantee, and often involve different foundations from the ones which are implied. Such a cosmopolitan order assumes a spontaneous identification of interests, which allows the creation and enforcement of rules necessary to ensure that exchanges benefit all parties. But how is this spontaneous identification to come about? At the very least there must be a way in which the undertakings that individuals make to one another are enforceable, so that trust and reasonable certainty can develop. It is hard to see how such an order can arise and persist without the support of states. If that is the case, the political question for neo-liberals becomes how they can ensure that states adopt a policy which supports rather than damages the liberal order.

This question has often been conceived rather narrowly within the parameters of a single nation-state, as though the global market did not exist. But once the existence of the global market is acknowledged, then neo-liberalism in one country becomes as futile as socialism in one country, since it is impossible to isolate a national economy indefinitely. This is particularly true of neo-liberalism and of Marxism because both are universalist doctrines – they believe they possess certain objective insights into the true and universal principles of social order which can be used in the remaking of the whole world, and their theoretical starting point is the whole human race rather than just part of it. These systems of thought are in principle antagonistic to nation-states, because their principles of order derive from the economy rather than from the state, and their notion of the economy is conceived in a universal rather than a particularistic manner. Nation-states are inherently particularistic.

The problems for the neo-liberal doctrine, however, go deeper. Neo-liberalism drew heavily upon the traditional free market analysis of the classical political economists, which argued for reducing state interference in the economy to a minimum in order to maximize wealth and economic liberty. In this conception the idea of the state as a night-watchman state, a state with minimal but still very important functions to do with the maintenance of law, public order, sound currency and the enforcement of contract, took hold. The state needed to be strong and decisive in first creating and then enforcing the conditions which made possible a space for relatively unhindered economic exchange. But how can the political will to keep the state to this minimalist conception of its role be ensured, particularly after the advent of democracy and the enfranchisement of the entire population? And, secondly, how can a liberal state ensure that its principles are extended to the international sphere, so that the economic space in which free exchange is possible is not artificially limited by national boundaries?

One traditional answer argued that it was a question of political agency. Liberals had to win the battle of ideas and the battle of organization, and defeat the enemies of the free society, whether on right or left, conservative or socialist. They had to ensure that the public philosophy adopted in every state was a liberal one. In this way the whole world could be converted to liberalism. Once they had experienced its benefits, the populations of particular states would not be likely to cast liberalism aside. The confidence of liberals in the ultimate victory of liberalism was based on their belief that only a liberal framework for modern society could provide prosperity and progress. Liberals thought they would triumph because their ideas were true, and those of their opponents were false.

Neo-Liberalism and the State

Neo-liberals still believe in the truth of liberal ideas, but in their assault upon all forms of collectivism sponsored by the extended state which developed in the twentieth century they incorporated modes of analysis drawn from the public choice school which are deeply pessimistic about the ultimate success of liberalism. Public choice analysis applied simple economic analysis to the state itself, arguing that the state should be disaggregated into the individual agents, the politicians and bureaucrats who composed it. All such agents were conceived to act like agents in the private sphere; they were self-interested in that they acted to maximize their benefits and to minimize their costs involved in any particular action. If they used the term 'public interest' to explain what they were doing it was simply a rhetorical device, used to cloak their self-interest.

The implications of self-interested and maximizing behaviour by politicians and bureaucrats were devastating. The idea of the state as a neutral guardian of the public interest was blown away. Instead of the state standing above society and mediating the conflicts between interests for the greater good, it was conceived as being infested by its own set of private interests, which, moreover, lacked many of the constraints which a competitive market-place provided. One of the main consequences was the enormous expansion of the state in the twentieth century. Internal pressures from democracy and external pressures from security combined to make politicians and bureaucrats, whatever their rhetoric, advocates of increasing the size of government. Larger budgets and greater administrative powers provided positive benefits to politicians and bureaucrats. Interest groups which supported the continued expansion of the state and state programmes became entrenched at every level of the modern extended state. The workings of democracy mean that voters have little incentive to consider the costs of new spending programmes which politicians put before them. Skilful politicians make the benefits of increased spending appear concentrated (on particular segments of the electorate) and the costs diffused. In this way democracy was seen as supplying a ratchet, in which, over time, the direction of public spending and taxation was always upward.

From this neo-liberal perspective the extended bureaucratic state has become an iron cage from which it is very hard to escape. Neo-liberal politicians, even if they are elected, will be confronted by the institutional and organizational reality of the state, and their self-interest will be to defend it and extend its powers and its budgets. Why should neo-liberal politicians be any different from any other politicians? If all individuals are self-interested, and if they act to maximize their benefits in the context in which they find themselves, then neo-liberal politicians would have to act *against* their interests in order to implement a neo-liberal programme. The neo-liberal political project seems to require a group of saints and altruists who understand that the public interest requires the dismantling of the extended state. But even if, contrary to the neo-liberal account of the world, such people were to be found, they could not be altruistic and saintly for a day. They would have to sustain it, and repel any attempt to return to an active state.

If this is the problem within a single nation-state, it gets still harder for the neo-liberal project when the implications of installing neo-liberal principles in the governance of the global market are considered. For again, what possible incentives can be imagined which would lead the politicians and bureaucrats of many different states to agree to establish and then police a framework which would ensure that the conditions for a liberal international order were met? Once again neo-liberals either have to believe that the principles and rules needed for co-ordination will arise spontaneously, and governments do not need to get involved; or they must put their faith in the far-seeing wisdom of a policy elite. Such a policy elite is easier to imagine in an authoritarian system than in a democratic one, since in the latter it faces pressures for more spending which arise through the competitive bidding of electoral competition between political parties. To reduce the extended state significantly, a neo-liberal political party would have to find ways of making reductions in state provision electorally popular. Reducing taxation is one such route, but the rhetoric is often very different from the substance, and the actual success of neo-liberal governments in rolling back the state have been small. The persistence of the extended state was one of the great facts of the twentieth century and one of its main legacies to the twenty-first.

Neo-liberals therefore hold an ideal of an unpolitical and even an anti-political world, but it can only be achieved through politics, and their analysis of how politics operates raises huge obstacles to the attainment of their ideal. The existence of a global market with many separate jurisdictions only makes the problem worse. Neo-liberals deal with this paradox in different ways. The least satisfactory is to believe that politics belongs to a set of malign forces which may yet be shrugged off by the power of the spontaneous order of the market, which has the capacity to be self-regulating, and to require no external political support. More realistic is the recognition that for the neo-liberal project to succeed it needs to be endorsed by the political elites in key states, as well as in the supranational agencies of the global market. This explains why one important strand of the discourse on globalization combines a strong attachment to national sovereignty with advocacy of complete openness to the global market. Only a national economy which is run according to neo-liberal principles can take full advantage of the opportunities created by globalization. The importance of national sovereignty becomes not to impose barriers on the global market and to try and insulate the national economy from it, but to ensure that the national economy is as integrated as much as possible with the global market, and that all domestic resistance to that integration is overcome.

What is interesting about this example is that it shows the way in which different principles of order can be combined in discourses on globalization. A strong attachment to territorial sovereignty does not preclude endorsement of a hyperglobalist account of the global market. Indeed, as far as the neo-liberal project is concerned it can be argued that it positively requires it, since the main alternative points in the direction of anarcho-capitalism and is wildly utopian. Only if the nation-state can be captured for neo-liberalism is there a prospect of the neo-liberal project being embedded both at the national and the global level. Similarly, although neo-liberals are not supposed to believe in forms of transnational governance other than those of global markets, the advantage for the neo-liberal project of colonizing the leading agencies of the global market with neo-liberals, and framing the hegemonic rules for the global market in line with neo-liberal principles, has understandable advantages, especially when the alternative is that many of these agencies might fall into the hands of interventionist liberals.

The key point for the argument of this book is that despite its disparagement of politics and its dream of a world without politics, neo-liberalism is an intensely political doctrine with a very strong sense of the different dimensions of the political and what has to be done to ensure that its priorities become political reality. It is hard to see how this could be otherwise. Far from the nation-state withering away, neo-liberalism has actually to accord it greater importance, and it does so in the name of globalization. It is the need to integrate the economy fully into the global market which makes the necessity of having a state which will facilitate that integration by removing obstacles and aligning domestic institutions with international ones so important. What is characteristic of this particular brand of neo-liberalism is that it combines the utmost fatalism about the nature of the global market with extreme voluntarism about the nation-state. The latter remains the fount of legitimacy, identity, meaning and purpose, but only so long as it accepts that its purpose is to subordinate all aspects of national life to the imperatives of globalization. The capacities of the nation-state are harmful if they are used in any direction other than in the interest of promoting integration of the national economy into the global market.

Against Universalism

In the 1970s and 1980s globalization became strongly associated with neo-liberalism, and its particular policy prescriptions: monetarism, deregulation, privatization and flexible labour markets. This policy package was not only adopted by several key states, including the United States and Britain, but also by many international agencies, particularly the IMF, the World Bank and the OECD, and a determined effort was made to export it to the rest of the world. This made globalization sometimes appear synonymous with neo-liberalism. The abandonment of national Keynesian policies by so many states was seen as a defeat for state autonomy and a sign of the new dominance of markets. Neo-liberal triumphalism soared to new heights after 1991 with the dismemberment of the Soviet Union. Many of its adherents had long suggested that not just communism and state socialism were discredited, but all forms of state intervention in the economy, including most forms of social democracy. They represented so many stages on the road to serfdom. What was required was the reassertion of the universal truth of the market order as the only feasible method of co-ordinating economic activity in modern society.

Globalization in this neo-liberal guise has been subjected to powerful criticism. One line of argument attacks the pretensions of neo-liberalism to be a universalist doctrine, and castigates it as a utopian system which its advocates wish to impose on all parts of the world, oblivious of the costs and destruction of societies and institutions which result. The main target here is Enlightenment doctrines which suggest that there is one universal dispensation appropriate for all human beings, and that its truths are captured by neo-liberalism. With the disappearance of Marxism as a serious player, liberalism in its particular variants is now the unchallenged last representative of the Enlightenment, with its emphasis on universal values and the supremacy of rational thought, and the ability to link virtue, reason and happiness.

For many critics of neo-liberalism, however, its universalism is a sham. Globalization is not bringing about a universal culture or a universal civilization. The greater connections between peoples associated with globalization do not prefigure any transcendence either of the state system or of quite separate civilizations and cultures. This obstinate pluralism of the world makes attempts to impose one universalist doctrine upon it and to transform all societies so that they fit a single pattern: imperialistic. They are only possible by using state power, the power of the hegemonic state – the United States – and its allies. But such an attempt, it argues, reveals globalization and neo-liberalism for what they are – not spontaneous unpolitical developments at all, but doctrines and discourses which serve the interests of the dominant power groups in the global market. In its reckless disregard of what makes states and cultures distinctive and its fatalism about the end of politics, neo-liberalism turns to power to impose its ideas when it meets resistance.

If the modern world is radically pluralist, in the sense that it is neither desirable nor feasible for it to be united by a single set of values and institutions, where does this leave globalization? The global market is, after all, a reality, and some means of governing it has to be found. Neo-liberalism proposes a way of governing it, which involves every state changing its internal arrangements to conform to the requirements of competition in global markets, and abandoning all forms of intervention. The steering mechanisms of this system lie in the global markets themselves, the myriad interactions between individuals which determine economic outcomes. The only task for states both at national and international level is to ensure a framework which allows those interactions to continue with minimal disruption or interference. The framework is entrusted to international agencies which are imbued with neo-liberal assumptions as to how the world works and how it should work. The end result is a cosmopolitan order beyond the reach of politics.

The opponents of universalism have an alternative. Against the idea of cosmopolitan order they emphasize the importance of territorial order; only this territorial order is in future to be based less on the nation-state principle, and more on an adaptation of the traditional international state system. This is to be a world if not of closed regionalism, at least of very definite blocs. Every bloc is founded upon a distinct civilization, and every civilization has a core state, which has the right to intervene in the affairs of other states within that civilization. In this way, the doctrine of distinct spheres of influence is resurrected. International agencies or the core state of another civilization have no right to intervene in the affairs of the member state of a different civilization. World order depends on the principle of territorial sovereignty being observed, and on any general rules – for example for economic exchange between blocs – being agreed between the core states of the leading civilizations, and not imposed on all states by the hegemon in the name of universal values.

Like the neo-liberal version of globalization this is a distinct *political* vision of world order. Whereas neo-liberals see globalization as our fate and celebrate national particularity only in so far as it is subordinated to it, for the anti-universalists the source of fate in the modern world lies in cultures and identities. It is these which establish the particularities which shape every individual and every society and make impossible universalist dreams. They have to be the foundation of any system of governance. The global market can only function without serious conflict if it is constructed on firm regional foundations. The world is naturally a world of blocs, and the skill of hegemony is to ensure that it is so governed as to minimize frictions and the threat of war.

The weakness of both universalism and anti-universalism is their fatalism. They endow certain structures, whether global cultures or civilizations, with such importance that they overpower the possibilities of agency and of politics. All agents can do is act in the shadow of these constraints. Their course is largely predetermined. But there are still political choices and alternatives. They are explored further in the final chapter.

4

The End of Authority

Another example of the fatalism which infests contemporary political discourse is the frequently heard claim that authority has been undermined and is close to collapse. There are two forms this fatalism has taken. The first is the fatalism of conservatives who assume that the present age is worse than some golden age in the recent past because respect for authority has collapsed. The second is the fatalism of those postmodernist and green radicals who believe that the basis for all forms of rational authority in modern society has been destroyed.

As with the end of history and the end of the nation-state, an end to authority would also threaten any conception of the political since some notion of authority is integral to it. To possess authority is to have the right to act in certain defined ways. The sources of authority are many and every claim to authority can be contested. One of the most important aspects of a society is, therefore, how authority is constituted, the different kinds of authority which exist, and how the relationships between them are determined. We speak of actions and commands being *authorized*, which means that they are perceived as legitimate. The greater the perception of legitimacy, the more likely it is that commands will be obeyed voluntarily and coercion, even if it is available, will not be needed. If, however, a command is not recognized as authoritative, there is no moral obligation to obey it (although it may well be prudent to do so). Those subject to it may try to evade it or subvert it.

Authority also is important in a broader sense. It relates not only to the commands and instructions of governments, but also to all those situations in which the acceptance of instruction and advice and the bestowal of trust are important. Authority reduces uncertainty and provides security. The sources of authority can come from many places: from habit, from inherited customs, from legal rules, from religion, from science, from personal charisma and from ideological doctrines. If all sources of authority were discredited, the shape of the political and the nature of the political order would become very hard to discern.

What does it mean then to speak of an end to authority? Everyone is against the authority they do not like, and there have always been fierce struggles in every society and culture to determine which claims to authority are justified or should take priority, for example between Church and State, Christianity and Islam, King and Parliament, capital and labour, or religion and science. The outcome of these struggles has determined the shape of politics, and the social and political institutions in each polity. But many of these struggles are never quite over, and their arguments continue to reverberate in our politics. Claims that authority is collapsing are often accompanied by fears that social order is breaking down, but what is often meant is that one particular kind of authority is threatened with extinction or rejection rather than all forms of authority as such. Much of the history of the modern period has been concerned with challenges to established forms of authority and attempts to substitute them with alternative sources of authority. This is not the same as trying to do away with authority itself.

One consequence is that there is a variety of narratives about the end of authority in our society, but different writers stress different forms of authority. Social conservatives decry the collapse of the authority rooted in traditional customs and modes of behaviour, and the tide of permissive and antisocial behaviour which is sweeping all before it, while progressives have lost much of their faith in the authority of many of the institutions which were intended to replace them. Both narratives can be fatalistic, but conservative fatalism is inscribed in the institutions and traditions of a society fast disappearing, while progressive fatalism derives from the existence of powerful organizational systems, such as modern science, whose claims to authority are no longer accepted, but whose power has become all-pervasive. For Max Weber, the conflict between traditional forms of authority such as religion and kinship and rational-legal forms of authority such as science and bureaucracy has been one of its defining features, while a third form – charismatic authority – has been intermittent but at times a threat to both. What is novel about the present time is that both traditional and rational-legal authority have substantially weakened, while the opportunities for the exercise of charismatic authority have increased.

Tradition and Society

Conservative narratives have always placed great weight on authority, because of their understanding of the importance of tradition in human societies. A traditional society is one in which present action is tightly circumscribed by customs which have been inherited from previous generations and whose origin and even rationale are unknown. Adherence to customs in a traditional society is so important because they are the means by which identity is established and affirmed. Changing the customs changes the identity of the society and the individuals who compose it, and this is why it is so fiercely resisted. Some intensely traditional societies, such as Japan before the Meiji restoration, or the Ottoman Empire, required a major political rupture for a new course to be established, which required the forcible suppression of old customs, symbolized by the outlawing of forms of dress. The Ottoman Empire was so averse to change that its word for innovation, *bida*, meant an event to be avoided if at all possible. The concept of fashion, of deliberate and frivolous change in dress and manners which had become strongly established in Europe by the middle of the eighteenth century, was completely alien.

All traditional societies have features in common with the Ottoman Empire, and they are features which are instantly understood and approved by conservatives. Such a conception of identity embodies a very clear idea of fate; human beings are tightly constrained by the traditions they have inherited. Their task is to live out the roles which their culture and traditions provide, not to question, initiate or innovate. Not all innovation, reform and originality are barred, even in the strictest traditional society, but their limits are very firmly set by the dominant customs prescribed by the tradition. The tradition also defines deviant behaviour, and prescribes punishments for it.

All societies were at one time traditional societies, and all societies remain in some sense traditional societies, since it is very difficult to conceive what a society which had no traditions would be like. Would we be able to recognize it as a society at all? The inheritance of customs and procedures, the habitual ways of doing things, which every society has, provide an essential framework within which individuals develop. If there were no traditions to absorb, it would be impossible for the individual to establish any kind of social identity. In order to establish an individual identity there first has to be a set of shared understandings about the different roles and objectives which characterize the society. Conservatives in general wish to conserve traditions and institutions which have been inherited and to resist or at least moderate change, on the grounds that what is known and tried is always preferable to what is unknown and untried, but also and perhaps more importantly because once continuity is given up identity becomes much harder to establish, and all kinds of pathologies and social disorders infect the polity.

One of the difficulties for conservatives in the modern era is that the advance of rational-legal authority, particularly as embodied in modern science, has threatened every traditional institution, creating a perpetual crisis of identity for both individuals and societies. Viewed from this angle, modernization is a process which constantly revolutionizes and overturns existing ways of doing things. It injects restlessness and insecurity into human affairs; everything has constantly to be reviewed, assessed and re-formed. If being conservative means anything, it has to mean resistance to modernization. But in any organization or society in the modern world, even some which place most emphasis on tradition, such as the Roman Catholic Church, that is a very uncomfortable position to sustain.

Conservatives in all societies find themselves having to adopt a series of holding positions; they seek to hold back the forces of progress for a time, before retiring to the next redoubt. But it is a strategy of delay and retreat, rather than advance, and it is hard to see how it could be otherwise, unless conservatives seek to leave the modern world altogether and seal their society off from contagion, as Islamic fundamentalists have indeed attempted to do. Conservatives have always sought 'shelter in our time', but they have always disagreed as to whether that is best secured by a policy of strategic concession to slow down the pace of modernization by acting so as to make concessions unnecessary. The second course requires repression, but conservative elites which have chosen it risk being overwhelmed in a great cataclysm, often, as in the case of the Soviet Union, after a belated switch to a policy of concession. But the problem for the strategy of concession is whether it ends up conserving anything at all, or merely connives in the slow destruction of all the traditions and forms of authority to which conservatives are attached.

One consequence of the general weakness of the conservative position in the modern era is that conservatives adopt characteristic devices in argument. One of these is the idea of a golden age of lost innocence and virtue, which is always located at some point in the past when identity was held to be secure and when traditions were not under threat, when nation-states had sovereignty, governments enjoyed legitimacy, citizens participated in public life, houses were left unlocked, men were employed in secure long-term jobs and people were anchored in traditional communities. The network of shared understandings was such that everyone knew their place and what was expected of them. Golden age conceptions are extremely prevalent, deeply conservative and mostly imaginary. These are reactionary utopias. They prevent clear thinking about change by exaggerating trends and by distorting the past.

The loss of such golden ages is one of the perennial staples of conservative discourse. In comparison with a golden age, the present always projects a scene of disorder, chaos and social collapse. Conservatives use the device of

the golden age to identify how particular forms of authority have been undermined, and the processes and agents
by which this has been accomplished. It therefore supplies
a ready list of enemies in the present which have to be
fought if the situation is not to deteriorate still further.
One of the favourite self-definitions of conservatives is
that they want to turn back the clock, and one of their
favourite complaints is that conservative parties and
governments fail in practice to turn it back even a few
seconds. But do conservatives really believe that the clock
could be turned back; that somehow the golden age of
their imagination could be restored?

One of their difficulties is that there is and can be no
definitive golden age, so the golden ages which are chosen
tend often to be quite near in time to the present. Golden
ages have sometimes been located as far back as the
European Middle Ages, but although such examples gain
in mystique, their practical relevance to the present is
sharply reduced. Golden ages which are quite recent,
however, are inherently flawed because whenever they are
examined their gilt quickly rubs off; they always had their
own crop of conservatives who expressed many of the
same complaints about this 'golden age' that their succes-
sors now make against the present. This is hardly surprising, since modernization has been a continuous process,
so that at any particular point in its progress conservatives
can always be found who decry it and point to the decline
of authority and the loss of identity and meaning.

A Non-Traditional Society

The modern era is therefore littered with golden ages and
with conservatives bemoaning their loss. The present is
no different in that respect. But many conservatives as

well as non-conservatives think that conservatives now
face a qualitatively new situation – the collapse of tradition
altogether with the emergence for the first time in human
history of a non-traditional society. A non-traditional
society is not the same as a society without tradition,
because such a society could not exist. There must always
be some customs, ways of behaving, social norms and
institutions which are inherited unreflectively from the
past. A society which was constantly remaking itself in
every particular would indeed be quite different from our
current experience.

The interesting question is not therefore whether a
society might arise which has no need of tradition at all,
but whether the role played by tradition in society might
shrink to the point that forces of change and modernization become dominant in shaping identities, roles and
expectations. The grounds for believing that something
like this is taking place are complex, since it is easy to
point out that one of the distinguishing features of
modernity is that right from the beginning there have
always been spheres of society which have become very
non-traditional in the way in which they have been organized. Certain aspects of the market economy stand out in
this respect, and the increasing detachment of market
relations from other social relationships, and the encouragement to apply rational techniques to the utmost in the
pursuit of profit, made this sphere the most dynamic, the
most subversive, the most modern, the most innovative
and the most free of all spheres of society. But it has also
been true of other spheres, including politics and culture,
in particular instances and at particular times.

The new claim is that these features of modernity which
related to specific sectors have been generalized to the
whole society, setting individuals free in a way which
would have been unimaginable to previous generations

but also at the same time leaving them dangerously adrift, and more prone to insecurity and uncertainty than ever before. The main characteristic of this non-traditional society is its value pluralism. It is not that it has no values; rather, it has a plethora of them and no easy means of choosing between them or establishing priorities. There are no longer authoritative accounts of how to live. The old authoritative accounts still exist, but for a growing number of people they are seen to have less and less validity. It is this situation which conservatives see as casting individuals adrift. Many still ultimately choose deep moral commitments, but for the conservative what is troubling is that the individual has to choose a moral way of life, rather than being automatically socialized into one. If moral fundamentalism and social traditions are one option among many, there is no reason why a large number of people should subscribe to them, and in any case a conservative understanding of tradition and authority means that the vast majority of citizens would have to make this choice in order for the society to conform to what conservatives believe it should be like.

True conservatives believe that certain kinds of choice are corrosive of individual identity and of authority. They need many areas to be off-limits for political debate, and off-limits therefore for modernization, rationalization and social engineering. Conservatives have to believe in the sacred, that there are certain matters which are too important to be compromised because they are the foundation stones of the national identity. A non-traditional society, by contrast, celebrates choice and indeed elevates it into an all-encompassing principle. It seeks to reduce tradition to a minimum by empowering individuals, making them self-reliant and controllers of their own fate. To the extent that it is against tradition, a non-traditional society is against the kind of fate which a traditional

society prescribes for the majority of its members. It wants
to liberate individuals, to help them to choose for themselves the kind of life they want, and to acquire the kind
of skills they need to lead it.

One consequence has been that the modernizing principle has now invaded all spheres of society and of the
state, including – perhaps most importantly – culture. The
collapse of the boundaries between high and popular
culture, the weakening of the idea of the university as a
critic of mass culture, in short the repudiation of all
traditional forms of authority in culture has helped generate some of the features of contemporary society, particularly the value relativism and the trivialization of culture,
the emphasis upon the immediate and upon self-gratifica-
tion which conservatives find most threatening. These
trends are at the heart of what is called postmodernism in
culture, but, as in other areas, many have pointed out how
postmodernity is not an alternative principle to modernity,
but, rather, represents heightened forms of it. In the
sphere of culture in particular it represents the triumph of
those quintessential modern processes.

It is an irony of contemporary politics that many of the
forces which have helped weaken and destroy traditional
forms of authority have been 'conservative' forces. This
stems from the current schizophrenia of conservatism
which tries to combine the discourse of neo-liberalism –
and even more bizarrely at times the language of libertarianism – with the more usual conservative emphasis upon
the sacredness of national institutions and national culture. The difficulty as conservatives have increasingly
discovered in the last few decades, is that it is impossible
to confine neo-liberal, still less libertarian, arguments
about free choice to the economic realm. The growing
importance of consumption and leisure in the advanced
capitalist economies make all such arguments about eco-

nomic choice very quickly into arguments about cultural choice as well. In these circumstances the pressure to subordinate all institutions and sectors to the forces of market competition has intensified – media, education, health, defence, policing, prisons: the list is growing. What hours and days shops should open, the availability of alcohol and drugs, access to pornography, privatization of schools and health care, abortion on demand: all these become issues which in a non-traditional society, it is argued, individuals need to decide for themselves, without the intervention of authority.

In embracing the market, conservatives embrace the most important part of the non-traditional society, the steering mechanism which is driving the rest, and in many countries parties from the right of centre have played a major role in helping to dismantle the defences of those institutions, particularly those in the public sphere which have stood out against the tide of modernization. The reason for this is that in neo-liberal discourse there is deep suspicion of authority and appeals to authority, because these are regarded as codes for state intervention and restrictions imposed upon free individual choice in a market order. 'Authority' is opposed to 'the market'. The former implies planning, paternalism, the imposition upon individuals of choices not their own. Weakening authority therefore becomes a way of liberating the individual. The opposition by neo-liberals to the extended state of the twentieth century led them to propose extending the modernizing processes of the market to state institutions themselves. The effects of this will be explored in the next chapter.

The problem for conservatives is how to put the genie back in the bottle, a genie they and their allies did much to help release. The notion that all the deleterious trends of the last few decades – from rising crime to Aids – can be traced principally to the cultural rebellions against authority of the 1960s fails to note the much larger role that has been played in allowing the market to become celebrated as the supreme mode of governance and organization in contemporary society. The institutional orders which had long acted as a counterweight to the market and as the effective repositories of tradition have been taken apart in several countries, and now the process is spreading to others. The result is, indisputably, greater openness and transparency, arguably greater efficiency, certainly more competition; at the same time there can be no denying that many forms of traditional authority have been weakened and discredited. In the absence of strong public institutions which shape the content, fix the hierarchy and determine the boundaries of the national culture, the way is open for it to be determined by the free interplay of companies and consumers. This levelling process, which conservatives so deplore, is a natural consequence of markets.

The consequence of the erosion of many traditional forms of authority is seen by conservatives as resulting in moral confusion. One response has been the growth of moral fundamentalism. In a society in which moral relativism and insecurity have grown, there are strong incentives for many individuals to take refuge in fundamentalist movements. Many conservatives have backed these movements or allied themselves with them, especially in the United States, but also in many other countries, especially in the Islamic world. The fundamentalists generally base themselves on a particular reading of their sacred religious texts and seek to impose a new authoritarian moral order which will roll back the tide of permissiveness and cultural pluralism, and re-establish a single identity and purpose for national life. Acknowledging that the moral consensus has been destroyed, they seek to reimpose one, by force if necessary.

In some Islamic countries which are also prepared to isolate themselves from the rest of the world such a new moral order has been established and may survive for some time. Many East Asian countries have also sought to combine a strong moral authoritarianism with rapid economic development, hoping to keep separate the modernization necessary to support economic growth from the modernization of culture and politics. There the attempt to combine a traditional society with a capitalist economy is still alive. But in the heartlands of capitalism, particularly the United States, the attempt looks forlorn. The traditional society has decayed too far to be easily resuscitated. In this situation moral fundamentalism manages to mobilize intense support amongst a minority, but has little prospect of building a majority consensus. The very intensity of its support for what it regards as core values therefore contributes to the fragmentation of the moral consensus in society and the undermining of the sense that any of the moral positions on offer are genuinely authoritative in a traditional sense.

Security

It might seem that the emergence of a non-traditional society and the retreat of traditional authority would spell the triumph of modernity and the enthronement of rational-legal authority throughout society, the displacement of religion and the elevation of science. But the weakening of tradition has not meant increasing acceptance of other forms of authority; rather, it has been part of a more general undermining of all forms of authority, including those which stem from the Enlightenment itself. The end of authority in this sense becomes a more universal phenomenon.

One reason for the weakening of all forms of authority lies in the increasing complexity of modern societies, brought about through the growing connections within the global market, but also through the impact of new technologies, new ways of organizing work and new forms of culture. The rational-legal institutions, such as companies and government agencies set up to manage these processes and which have been responsible for their acceleration and extension, have created a world in the last two hundred years which is significantly different from any human society that has previously existed. It has made tradition far less valuable as a guide to behaviour and as an anchor of security and identity, but it has also undermined the claims of the rational-legal to legitimacy, because the world which has been created, far from providing emancipation, has provided new forms of enslavement. The iron cage of modern life provides hitherto unimaginable standards of living for a minority of the world's peoples, but at the same time has increased competition, insecurity and risk.

Some of the claims made for the increasing level of risk in our societies are exaggerated, and often rely again on the assumption of a mythical golden age somewhere in the past, a time when risks were much lower than they are now. Part of the reason for this lies in a particular view of the twentieth-century welfare state – that it greatly reduced insecurity from unemployment, sickness, old age and disability, while at the same time reducing the effects of poverty by providing a floor income below which no one should fall. In the last twenty years, however, there has been a preoccupation with the return of old forms of insecurity and the rise of new ones, and with the increasing risks which individuals and their families face as a result.

Conservatives often contrast a present time of heightened insecurity and increasing risk with an imaginary past when there were no risks, or much reduced ones. Much of the popular discussion of crime or drugs or new diseases, for example, tends to imply that there was once a golden age when these things were not serious problems. Similarly, the period of the 1950s and 1960s is often treated as a golden age in terms of economic performance, particularly as regards unemployment and inflation. But in a longer perspective this period looks decidedly aberrant, the product of special circumstances rather than especially wise and effective policy. What is true is that the nature of risk and insecurity does change, in particular the perception of them. The consequences of the weakening of tradition and the availability of new sources of information, and the immediacy of events from around the world due to new forms of communication all combine to make contemporary societies much more aware of certain kinds of risk.

Increasing risks and insecurity might mean only that there were deficiencies in the way in which the rational-legal institutions of contemporary societies were organized, and that appropriate reforms would enable them to provide solutions to all these problems, as it was claimed solutions were found to the problems of nineteenth-century capitalism. What is required is better policy, more effective implementation, better monitoring and evaluation of the results, better communication between governments and corporations and the people. But the problems may go much deeper. There is a pervasive malaise about the performance of all the bureaucratic structures which dominate contemporary societies, a lack of trust in leadership and a cynicism about management which is deeply corrosive of authority. The complexity of the problems with which they are dealing outrun solutions, so the increasing temptation is to resort to modern media to provide comfortable messages and to divert attention away from the lack of substance that any collective agency is able to provide in terms of delivery. One obvious effect of this in relation to politics has been the growing importance of personalities, because in a world in which other sources of authority are wearing thin, saleable personalities increase in importance. Using charisma, or at least the modern commercial version of it, as the main way to legitimate the policies of states and corporations has become more and more pronounced.

The problem which has been identified by many different observers is how individuals can find security and identity in a world drained of meaning by the weakening of traditional forms of authority, and forced increasingly into iron cages of technical legal rationality to which individuals feel little loyalty and from which they derive little satisfaction. If these trends were true, the result would be an increasingly restless, mobile, competitive and unhappy population.

Science

It was not supposed to be like this. Science in particular was, from the beginning, the great hope of modernity. Scientific rationality would gradually banish error and superstition and establish the institutions and the procedures by which society would become a learning society, proceeding by trial and error to discover the best available solution for whatever problem had to be confronted. Elaborate methods were developed to provide a calculus of how the public good might be assessed, while others preferred to avoid any centralized determination, leaving it instead to the free flow of choices and interactions in a market order. But despite these disagreements on means, there was a widespread consensus that scientific rationality would enable human societies to make progress, to become wealthier, freer, happier, better educated and healthier.

It is hard to disagree with the fact that, compared with two hundred years ago, there has been a considerable improvement in most, if not all, of those indicators, at least for the citizens of the rich societies of the West. But there is also undeniably a pervasive unease about the future and about the ability of human societies to cope, and a large part of this unease derives from the institutionalization of science itself. Science is not just a particular form of knowledge but a social enterprise. Its principles are embedded not only in the methods employed by research teams in laboratories, but also in the organizational forms of the modern economy and modern state. Science has become deeply integrated with both, and as a result it is hard to stand outside the process and view it as a whole.

The problem can be simply stated. It is the idea of a runaway world, in which the very processes which have brought about the conquest of disease, the raising of living standards and the provision of opportunities now threaten to take them all away, because of the effect of the industrialization process on the ecology of the planet. Some of the original fears were voiced by the Club of Rome at the end of the 1960s, when it pointed to the unsustainable nature of escalating levels of resource use when combined with population growth. Some of these concerns were popularized as the idea that certain non-renewable resources would simply run out. That idea was rejected, because it divorced the conception of a resource from the economic circumstances in which it might be exploited. Its critics argued that the reserves of any resource are not finite in a strict physical sense; it depends on the relationship between the cost of extraction and the price that can be charged.

The dwindling of finite resources could in principle be solved by changes in relative prices and adjustment of patterns of use. Much more troubling, however, has been a second set of problems which ecologists have highlighted. These relate to irreversible changes in the ecology of the planet to which current industrialization processes may lead. Chief among these are global warming and the threats to biodiversity. This is still an issue of sustainability, but the focus has shifted on to the difficulties in disposing of the waste products of the industrial system, and the wider effects many of them are having upon the environment.

Disposing of the waste products of industrialism in ways which do not do irreversible damage to the planet's ecology is a pressing political problem, but again it is in principle soluble, provided sufficient support can be generated for some of the radical solutions which will be necessary. But the solutions have to be found within existing industrial societies. No one thinks it credible, even if some think it desirable, that the great engine of modernity could be put into reverse, and that human societies could go back to much simpler forms of organization, which would once again be in harmony with the natural environment. For such a move to work it would have to be agreed across all societies and within societies. Neither is at all likely. The implication is that if the ecological dangers are to be averted for future generations, the solutions have to be found not by retreating from science and technology but by intensifying them. Modern science which has created the problem has to be enlisted to solve it.

In principle, this is possible, although the history of many technologies up to now shows that it takes time for their harmful side-effects to be recognized. The problem with the trajectory of modern societies is that they are having to run to stand still, and the pace is accelerating all the time. Another difficulty lies in the close ties between scientific research and modern companies. During the twentieth century science was incorporated into the production process, and became a major force of production. The proliferation of research laboratories and the commercialization of research have created an enormous engine for the development of new technologies, but also put a strong emphasis on the commercial success of new products. This is posing major problems for regulation, as the example of genetically modified food, developed by the research arms of some of the major transnational biotech companies, has made abundantly clear. The GM food issue also illustrated the problem that now exists for science. Despite very strong scientific assurances as to the safety of existing GM food, the public in many countries has not been reassured. The authority of science is no longer sufficient in cases like these. Stronger guarantees are required, but none is available, because science can only deal in probabilities and make provisional judgements in the light of the available evidence, and some of the issues involved in the GM food controversy could never be resolved in this way.

There are still deeper problems for the future, which are less easy to resolve because they strike at the heart of the value systems of existing societies. The accelerating pace of scientific knowledge will create huge dilemmas. The potential of new medical technologies, in particular those concerned with genetic engineering, such as cloning, have profound implications for all traditional ideas about fate. They potentially strike at one of the key ideas about human beings – that the genetic inheritance of each individual is outside human control; what people are born with is regarded as in part a lottery, which cannot be altered, and provides the basic conditions within which we must live our lives. If the new genetics means that there can be interventions either to choose or to change the genetic inheritance we are born with, effecting radical changes in the lifespan, the genetic characteristics, abilities and behaviour of individuals, then the most searching questions will be asked of our existing societies and their moralities, since such possibilities would change human experience and our understanding of human nature. At present these issues have only arisen in mild forms. But the potential has been glimpsed, and the debates on abortion and contraception show how controversy can surround new medical technologies. Controversy will be multiplied many times over when some of the next generation medical technologies become available. It *is* a question of 'when'. Even if one country were to shut down all research into a particular area, the diversification of the scientific enterprise into so many centres around the world ensures that the research would proceed elsewhere and the knowledge would at some stage become available. Once available, it will be very hard for access to be denied in open political systems. But once access is granted, societies may be altered permanently. The many new expectations, demands and conflicts which will be raised will be extremely difficult for any existing political system to handle. But if they cannot be handled through politics, they cannot be handled at all.

5

The End of the Public Domain

The final example of fatalism declares the end of the public domain. In doing so it strikes right at the core of politics, for if there is no public domain, no public interest, no civic engagement, no public opinion, no public agency, one of the major dimensions of the political would have disappeared. Yet at the beginning of the twenty-first century the public domain in its different manifestations is in some trouble, and there has been no shortage of writers to declare that it is moribund and to welcome the approach of a new age in which older conceptions of the public have no place. Once again, however, as with so much of the writing on endism, the debate suffers from being too foreshortened. There is rarely any historical depth in the analysis and a tendency to exaggerate what are undeniably important and interesting trends into sweeping judgements that politics is dead and cannot recover.

The End of Government

One of the most persistent forms of this writing involves speculation about an end to government. Dreams of an end of government are not new. They have long been a part of the western political imagination, and numerous political thinkers, including Karl Marx, have looked forward to the withering away of the state. But whereas Marx acknowledged that the business of administration would still have to be performed and that therefore, in some form, government would be necessary in the classless society, many contemporary accounts foresee the displacement even of government. One of the most influential forms of this writing is to be found in libertarianism and also in many strands of neo-liberalism, for even though neo-liberals accept the need for a minimal state, it is a grudging acceptance, and the tenor of their writing is to wish that the world could be made free of government and of politics, from which flow most of the evils with which the world is afflicted.

What evidence is there that government might be withering away? As with the withering away of the nation-state, a casual perusal of the current scene seems to point in the opposite direction. There appears to be increasing rather than diminishing activity by governments. The case to the contrary rests on highlighting certain significant trends in the way government is organized throughout the world, such as the diminishing of public sectors through the privatization of public assets, deregulation of private sectors, and the drive to cut taxation and reduce state funding for the expansion of welfare. It is generally acknowledged, however, that as yet even the most radical governments have at best halted the growth of the state; they have not succeeded in reversing it. More central to the argument, perhaps, is the idea that the state has been 'hollowed out' through the adoption of the doctrines of 'the new public management', among which are the separation of policy advice from policy implementation, and the organization of the latter through public agencies, public/private partnerships or private companies; the encouragement of internal markets; and a readiness to contract out services and to use competition to encourage greater efficiency. The adoption of the new public management is an important development in public administration, but whether it is leading to an end of government is highly doubtful. It is government by other means.

In some of the writing on globalization and the information revolution the argument is advanced that the pace of development in the leading sectors of the new global market is undercutting the whole basis on which the extended state of the twentieth century was based. The nation-state, it is said, is no longer the appropriate site for steering the economy, and is losing its ability to regulate economic activity and to tax it. With the dwindling of its fiscal base the state will be forced constantly to reassess its priorities and its programmes, and to accept a much reduced role.

In some neo-liberal versions of this scenario, popular with the hyperglobalists, the process of change is driven by the self-regulating global market itself. A point is reached where the market order throws off the unwelcome tutelage of the state. The steering functions which the market requires are all provided by the market itself. If there is a need for a particular service, the gap in the market will be spotted by an entrepreneur and the service provided. If the service is not provided, that seems to indicate that there is no need for it. From this perspective, comprehensive deregulation of the global market would allow market agents to decide for themselves what forms of self-regulation they require. Many libertarians go further: they question the need for states to have a monopoly in the issue of currency, so they would abolish central banks, as well as interventionist supranational agencies such as the IMF and the World Bank. If the global market is allowed to develop to the full, then government becomes redundant.

Governance

In this discourse, as in some others about the state and government, the attempt by governments in the past to centralize power and to exert control over everything within their jurisdiction is seen as ultimately stifling of enterprise and initiative. States by themselves on this view are unable to steer an economy adequately; they are too inflexible and rigid. A much more diversified pattern of governance than that which governments can supply needs to be inaugurated. The passage from government to governance has become one of the central narratives in recent writings on politics. The term 'governance' has been resurrected in order to suggest the range of steering mechanisms by which societies are governed. Government is one of those mechanisms and clearly on any reckoning remains a most significant one, but it is by no means the only one. The mode of governance employed by governments tends to be a hierarchical organization with a clear specification of duties and chain of command and responsibility. Other modes of governance such as markets and networks co-ordinate and steer action by different means.

What is valuable in the governance perspective is that it reminds us of certain factors involved in the way societies are governed which were overlooked when there was such concentration upon the state and upon the notion of sovereignty. The Westphalian model of sovereignty was always misleading if interpreted in too absolutist a fashion, as though the only source of power and influence were states. During the nineteenth century the predominant trends in social science and in political thought tended to play down the role of the state and concentrated instead on the forces remaking society – politics and the state were often relegated in both Marxism and liberalism to the status of a superstructure, a reflection rather than a determinant of the forces shaping the modern world.

Governance brings attention back to the complex ways in which societies are governed and stable patterns of social interaction established. In particular it focuses on all the non-state networks and markets which connect individuals without the mediation of government or corporate bureaucracies. But all this is a long way from apocalyptic claims that government could disappear. On examination, most of these claims do not stand up. There is often a failure to distinguish national government from government more generally. At the national level it is true that certain state functions which in recent decades were performed by national governments have been transferred either to supranational bodies or to devolved bodies. A complex pattern of multi-level governance is evident, particularly in the European Union, where different governing functions are allocated to different levels. The principle of subsidiarity requires each function to be performed at the most decentralized level possible.

What multi-level governance does not mean is any necessary diminution in the amount of government. Indeed, many defenders of the idea of undiluted national sovereignty in the European Union regard the growth of multi-level governance as adding tiers of government, and increasing the amount of governing by governments. Their support for the nations to remain self-governing is so that each nation can decide for itself the regulatory burden it wishes to impose upon itself. Advocates of multi-level governance, however, point to the growing interdependence of national economies and the advantages of creating more unified economic spaces operating under a common set of rules. The adoption of such rules has been seen as part of a more general move from the interventionist nation-states of the recent era to a regulatory state, many of whose functions are exercised at a supranational level, both regional as in the case of the EU and global as in the case of the WTO. This move to a regulatory rather than an interventionist state does not portend the end of government. It may even mean an increase in government, but not necessarily government at the national level.

This change might still be held to imply that power is drained away from national governments and that the state loses a great deal of its former importance. The national state would become a weak state, lacking the capacities to achieve its goals, because many of these capacities would have been transferred elsewhere. But this fear too seems strange when closely examined. The strong states of the future, the states which develop the capacities to achieve their goals, are likely to be those which develop successful cooperation with other states. This is increasingly one of the most important capacities which states need to have. The idea that states can increase their strength by isolating themselves from other states is odd. It only makes sense in a neo-liberal discourse which sees the criterion of state strength as the ability to subordinate the national economic policy to the requirements of the global market.

A popular analogy is that lean companies should be the role model for lean states. Just as companies have learned to shed subsidiaries and concentrate on their core business, so states need to do the same. But it is much harder to determine what the core business of the state is than it is for companies, partly because so many different roles are in fact performed by the state, but also because exactly what the core business of the state should be has been at the heart of political debate for centuries. No one is actually in favour of a bloated state; there are just different accounts of what the core functions of the state are and what they should be. Understanding government in the context of governance means recognizing that many of the tools which governments use belong to one particular mode of governance, and that there are other ways of coordinating and steering societies which may possibly be superior in achieving whatever goals government has. The important point is that the balance between different modes of governance is a key issue for politics, since all modes of governance, including markets, require political legitimation and support.

Public and Private

What this simple point reflects is the poverty of our current language in describing the state and its relationship to the rest of society. One of the most common ways of talking about the state concerns the boundaries between the public sector and the private sector, which suggests that there is a zero-sum relationship between the two, so that if the state is expanded, the public sector grows and the private sector contracts. This leads to the familiar language of rolling back the state, much loved by certain politicians, as though the state was like an immense carpet which suffocates everything it covers. This idea of the state as an imposition, a burden, reflects one way in which the state is experienced, but it also ignores others. The state is often identified with government, and also with the public. But government is at most one part of the state, a particular organizational means for delivering publicly agreed policies.

Similarly, the public domain is a category much wider than government. How the public sphere and public activity are defined are crucial issues in every polity. What needs to be done in the present era is to disentangle the idea of the public domain from the much more limited concept of the public sector, with which it has been identified for too long. The distinction between public and private remains crucial in understanding the nature of the public domain, but properly understood the public domain should not be confused with government or what government directly controls. It is the sphere of common affairs and the discussion of common problems, in which 'public' and 'private' actors alike participate.

The End of Civic Engagement

Beyond an end to government there has also been much speculation about an end to civic engagement in the public domain. The decline in participation in public affairs among citizens is the trend most often pointed to, reflected in party membership, voting and public meetings, as well as a more general decline that has been observed in citizens joining voluntary associations in civil societies. The idea that there has been a pronounced decline in civic engagement and public awareness is part of a wider critique of modern society in which specific public spaces and public activity are perceived to be under threat. The pursuit of private pleasures is seen as all-pervasive and, it is argued, steadily undermines any sense individuals possess of the polity as in some sense their polity. An understanding of the polity as a republic – *res publica*, public affairs, a space for public action and public speech – was always difficult to preserve in the context of mass electorates and complex societies, but even the little that was preserved now seems under threat.

One of the causes of this state of affairs is held to be the circumstances of modern mass politics and the role played by the new media. It took some time for the character of mass democratic politics to be understood, and for politicians to start acting accordingly, so that for a long while many politicians still believed that their task was political education and political leadership through such organizational means as the mass party and the mass meeting. Only gradually did it become apparent that the majority of the electorate would never become active in political parties and would never make the effort to acquire serious political knowledge. The ability of political leaderships to cut themselves off from their political parties and appeal directly to the electorate through the mass media, particularly television, proved irresistible. It meant that all the marketing techniques pioneered elsewhere could be employed in making candidates and their parties electable, and that electoral politics could become a battle of images and soundbites rather than a battle of arguments. Politicians became focused on the main issue, which was how they could maximize their vote, and this meant ensuring that their messages and stances were perfectly attuned to the voters who counted most in the election. The latest example of this application of professional techniques to electioneering has been focus groups, which all parties now use in order to improve the presentation of their message.

The result of this new media politics is, its critics allege, a concentration on presentation rather than substance, and on personalities rather than issues. Electoral politics becomes a spectacle, a gladiatorial combat between the party leaders, which intermittently engages the electorate's attention, but which has little deeper meaning for them. With the narrowing of political debate, as all parties seek to define and then occupy the centre ground, so interest in the outcome often dwindles and fewer people bother to vote, because they cannot see it makes a difference to them, and fewer too come to see the act of voting as an important expression of their identity. On both counts turnout at elections is set to fall. This process has gone furthest in the United States but the trend is also becoming visible in Europe. Similarly, this process is also deeply discouraging to many of the people who used to be active members of political parties, because their role in party decision-making is much diminished; a vote in the choice of the leader is the one area where ordinary members have been given more say, whether through primaries or through direct election. But policy-making has mostly been taken away altogether from members. They are consulted but they no longer have an opportunity to change policy.

These trends are reinforced by more general threats to the public domain. Public-service broadcasting, where it exists, is everywhere under attack, and with the explosion of new technological possibilities for the media in the digital age, there has been increasing pressure to end the privileges which public-sector broadcasting enjoys. The provision of in-depth news and comment on politics is therefore threatened, but its axing can easily be justified on the basis of audience figures. Similarly, the process known as 'dumbing down' has spread through the quality broadsheet press, while weekly and quarterly journals struggle to survive. As a result both of their declining numbers and the intensification of academic specialization in the universities, the class of public intellectuals whose special function is public speech and the definition and construction of the public and the political appears to be in retreat in every country. On this kind of reading of current trends, the public domain is everywhere shrinking, to be replaced by dull technocratic administration on the one hand and meaningless media spectacles on the other. The result is a withdrawal from public engagement; more and more people concentrate on their private lives and private pleasures.

Participation and Accountability

That there are trends which point in this direction are undeniable; many of the hopes about democracy have not been fulfilled. Knowledge about politics has remained concentrated and active citizenship beyond voting and paying taxes remains rare. But the characterization is also flawed because implicitly it draws upon a model of political involvement and political participation which has not existed in modern times and never could exist. Much of the force behind this comes from the ideal represented by the polities of the ancient world, particularly some of those in Greece, where the public domain had a status much higher than the private, and in which public action and public speech were prized as being what made men distinctively human. This polity was certainly not inclusive (women, like slaves, were confined to the private sphere and denied rights), but for those who were citizens there was an ideal of the public domain which has continued to resonate in the political imagination down to our own time, and its passing is still much regretted.

Aside, however, from the question of whether such a model could ever have been adapted to the much larger-scale societies of the modern world, the other reason why the model is inappropriate is that from its earliest beginnings the modern period has been characterized by a very different understanding of the relationship between the public and the private. In this understanding the private has taken precedence. The purpose of the polity is to promote and facilitate the attainment of private desires and needs. This has not suddenly changed; it has always been the trajectory of modernity. It is against this background that changing forms of participation should be viewed. It is a mistake to take certain forms of participation which became established in the first half of the twentieth century and imagine that they represent some kind of standard against which the present can be judged. Forms of participation change, and the understanding of what the public is and how it can be realized also change. There are obviously trends which threaten the public and the idea of a public space, but the way in which new forms of participation and new public agendas emerge need also to be acknowledged. New technologies associated with the information revolution are opening up new ways in which citizens might participate in the future, which fit the new kinds of community and social interaction which are emerging. Old forms of social capital may decline, but new ones are often being created at the same time. There is nothing automatic about this, and there are sometimes real losses. But the process is never just one way. New opportunities involving new ways of extending participation will arise, and should be seized.

The fatalism which is inherent in the idea of the end of the public domain is similar to the fatalism present in all the endisms discussed in this book. Their chief flaw is not that they fail to highlight signal dangers but that they present developments as a unilateral trend which can only have one outcome. But there are always many more possibilities than that, and one of the purposes of politics is to ensure that those possibilities can be debated, explored and tested. The observation that political elites seek to centralize power and manipulate voters and restrict public debate is hardly novel. Elites have generally behaved in this way. There has always been a tension between the hierarchy and secrecy of the modern state and its characteristic forms of rule, and a culture and politics of openness and accountability. This tension takes new forms in every period and the present period is no different. But the idea that we face some imminent and final closure of the political because political parties are losing members, voter turnout is dropping and political leaders are marketed more brazenly than ever before is not convincing. The struggle to improve and to deepen democracy is never-ending, and as long as democratic forms themselves survive, every attempt to limit democracy will encounter resistance. There is no guarantee that resistance will be successful or that there is any inevitable progress in the way in which societies develop. They can go backwards as well as forwards. But in evaluating possibilities we ought not to think that something extraordinary and cataclysmic is happening at the present time which marks a watershed in human affairs.

The End of the Public Interest

The relationship of politics to the public domain is bound up with the question of the public interest. Is there a public interest which is separate from private interest? Many political theorists have dismissed the idea as being without value. When politicians talk about acting in the public interest, or taking the public interest into account, this is taken to be simply a cloak for private interest. Politicians seek to make what they do legitimate by claiming to act in the name of the public, but their real motives and intentions are based on calculations of what will advance either their own interests or the interests of those they represent.

Claims that there is no such thing as the public interest have been advanced most strongly in recent years by the public choice wing of neo-liberalism. Public choice applies simple economic models and economic assumptions to the analysis of politics, and seeks to strip away the pretensions and illusions with which politics surrounds itself. If all that exists are individuals and their interests, then it does not matter whether an individual is a consumer or a politician: the analysis of their behaviour will be similar. All individuals are assumed to be rational and to maximize their utility, so they make choices which maximize their benefits and minimize their costs. Costs and benefits are subjective and ultimately only knowable by the individual. Applied to politics, these assumptions mean that concepts such as the public interest and enlightened government or government for the good of the people have no meaning. The government has to be disaggregated into the individuals who compose it – the politicians and bureaucrats – all of whom are pursing their own private interests and seeking to maximize their (subjective) utility. The consequence is a system which produces highly damaging outcomes, because the political market is severely distorted by very imperfect competition and the absence of any serious budget constraint. The result is that politicians and bureaucrats are able to expand their budgets and the scope of their activities with few checks. This leads to outcomes which promote their interests but at the expense of everyone else.

Neo-liberals see almost nothing good in politics; it is the source of most of the evils in the world and therefore needs to be reined back as much as possible. A politics-free world would be a much better place. The argument is highly reductionist. It seeks to uncover the private interests which lurk behind every profession of public service. The argument is not that individuals are necessarily naturally wicked (although some think they are) but that unless individuals are placed within a firm framework of rules which disciplines them and channels their behaviour they will behave in ways which advance their interests at the expense of others. The problem with politics and the public domain is that it is impossible to devise rules which make the political market as competitive as normal commercial markets. The implication is that the political market, if not closed down altogether, should at least be restricted as much as possible, so that it can do least damage.

Neo-liberalism vigorously attacks all notions of the public good, of public altruism, of enlightened paternalism, or neutral and omniscient government. In this (if in not much else) it resembles those strands of Marxism which also argued in a reductionist manner that since in a class society it was impossible for the state to be neutral between classes, protestations that the state represented some universal interest were bogus, and always a cover for a particular class interest. Indeed, the state only existed to protect a particular constellation of class interests. All state policies were directly class policies in the sense of serving the interests of a particular class. There was no independent space for politics.

The best objections to these neo-liberal and Marxist arguments have come from within neo-liberalism and Marxism themselves. Reductionist arguments are often striking and compelling, but in the end fallacious. They are right to question the automatic attribution of terms such as public, altruistic, enlightened and impartial to public policy. But they offer a very one-sided and incomplete account of the public sphere and the state. In particular, they cannot distinguish between policies and action which may serve particular individual interests, and actions which set frameworks and establish general rules which then allow individuals to pursue a variety of interests. If their account of politics and the state were correct, it would just be a spoils system; levels of corruption and abuse of public office would be endemic. Some political systems and states are indeed like that. But why are they all not like that? The fact that they are not argues strongly for a notion of the public interest which is separable from the private interest of the participants in the public domain.

The public interest is distinct as a concept from the notion of a public good where this is conceived as something objective and knowable through the exercise of reason, and therefore in principle accessible by an elite. This classical conception of the good and of knowledge are different from modern conceptions, just as the ancient world's conceptions of the public and the private were different. Private originally meant withdrawal from public life and signified deprivation. The enlargement of the private sphere as one of intimacy and independence and the sphere of the market in opposition to the state are the work of modern times. The conflation of public and state was a particular phenomenon of the twentieth century. Private enterprise became opposed to public enterprise – i.e. state enterprise – although it would have been as appropriate to counterpose public enterprise (publicly quoted limited liability companies owned formally by their shareholders) to state enterprise (firms wholly owned by the state).

In the classical conception of the public good there is no place for interest. The idea of a public interest as opposed to a public good could only arise in a society in which private interest was perceived as the foundation of the social order. The public interest was constructed by Bentham and the utilitarians as the aggregate of individual interests. But even if we accept the principle that society exists in order to facilitate the private pursuit of happiness by its members, there is still the problem of how all the individual projects for happiness can be kept from colliding. Unless it is assumed that the necessary institutions and rules will spontaneously arise, or that certain individuals will see the need for certain services which other individuals then purchase, it is hard to see how the need for the state or for public bodies which take a long-term view of the general arrangements of the society can be avoided.

The public interest cannot be derived either from an objective conception of the public good or from the spontaneous pursuit by individuals of their private interests. But that does not make the conception meaningless; the attempt to define it becomes one of the most important aspects of modern politics. What is at stake in the conception of the public interest is not only how public and private are defined and the relationship between them, but also the definition of the public domain, and beyond that the conception of the political realm, and the criteria and values which are appropriate for formulating and evaluating public policy and public actions. This means that the public interest cannot be a fixed thing; it is always contested and in process of negotiation. What it is in any particular society or period will be determined by the strength of different interests and pressures, by historical legacies, by events, by ideological argument and political leadership – in short, by politics.

Such a conception will not still the complaints that the term is vague and can mean both everything and nothing. What it depends upon is the development of a particular discourse about the public domain, a particular ethos of public service and public responsibility, and particular criteria for rational discussion of the public interest. A great deal of the contemporary discussion of the public interest revolves around fairness, how to frame rules which embody it and how to deal with deviations from it. Ideas of equal treatment and due process, as well as specific criteria for allocating resources and determining eligibility are central, therefore, to identifying the public interest.

Such a process is always vulnerable to corruption by the venality of public officials or the pursuit of special interest parading as general interest. In an established democracy, however, there is an accumulation of institutions and agencies which are imbued with a public interest outlook. The public interest is not biased towards one particular outcome, such as an expanded state. The minimal state is also a version of the public interest, which sees the public interest as being best secured through the state confining its activities to a few core functions. But this still defines an important public domain and acknowledges the need for public criteria and public values.

The argument that politics is no longer relevant and is dwindling in importance and relevance in a world whose fate will be determined by globalization and technology fails to understand the particular contribution politics makes and has always made. A world of hyper-globalization and rampant technology would seem to require more consideration of the public interest rather than less, more attempts to construct frameworks in which the impact of both processes can be monitored and the benefits shared. New examples crop up every day, such as the argument over whether research laboratories which crack part of the genetic code should be allowed to patent their results and charge fees to anyone who wishes to use them, or whether such research belongs to the public domain and should be made freely available to all researchers. This is a classic public interest issue; it is also an issue which goes to the heart of the governance of the global market. Determining what is the public interest in this case means deciding whether the decoding of the genetic code is so important a scientific breakthrough discovery that it must be claimed as common property and not appropriated by private interests. The issue will be contested at first legally, but the courts in Europe and the United States may take a different stance. If they do, then the question of the public interest would move from the courts to the governments, which would have to consider whether to sign an international agreement to ensure the genetic code remains in the public domain and is publicly accessible.

Political questions such as these will multiply in the years ahead. The need for an active and open political debate, and for the preservation of a healthy public domain, would seem obvious. Governments do not control this debate, although at times they seek to manipulate it. What is called the end of government or the end of politics is often no more than a judgement that governments are less powerful than they were. A revolution in government is taking place and many of the old conceptions of the public domain are no longer very useful or accurate. Clear thinking about the principles which should define the public domain are urgently needed. But the public domain itself is not about to disappear.

6

Politics

Although one of the central claims of some forms of endism is that the era of the great meta-narratives is over, endism itself belongs to these narratives and bears the impress of them. It understands change in the same way that they do, in terms of trends rather than cycles. Its belief that a qualitatively new stage in human development has been reached which allows the period of modernity of the last two hundred years to be left behind is a quintessential modernist conception. According to this narrative, in the last two hundred years trends in population growth, trade, economic output, technological innovation and media and cultural exchange have been both upward and cumulative. Together they have created the interdependent global market. Progress has not been even, and there have been sharp setbacks and declines, often as a result of wars and economic depressions, but the upward momentum has always resumed. New stages of social development have been achieved which do not reproduce the past. Instead of endlessly repeated cycles, human experience of social change in the last two hundred years has been progressive. Change moves history on, rather than round, which means that while some things stay constant, others are entirely new in the experience of generations.

The writing on endism does not challenge this view; it endorses it. Other cultures, including past western cultures, have had different conceptions of change. A real challenge to the way in which time and space are conceived in the twenty-first century would be a revival of a cyclical view of change. But for most forms of endism the emphasis upon scientific knowledge and technological innovation remains central. The new information revolution is the catalyst which is causing the demise of so many of the institutions and practices of the last hundred years, as its consequences percolate through all social institutions. But this revolution is in principle no different from other revolutions which have occurred before in the modern era.

Some of the writing on endism can be read in this way, as offering an account of the new stage of historical development which is upon us, clearing the ground for new thinking, new forms of life, new institutions, new relationships – a new economy. Every revolution, every generation announces itself by declaring liberation from the past, a new start, an open future, an end of history. Is the writing on endism any different? It may at times exaggerate, but perhaps this is necessary to shock and jolt us out of our complacency, to make us aware that the earth is moving, that something qualitatively different is happening.

The celebration of the new is an essential part of modernity; and as always it tends to generate extremes of wild optimism and deep pessimism. Both are to be found in the writing on endism. The more enthusiastic proponents of globalization, for example, believe that a new stateless cosmopolitan order is arising which will sweep away the detritus of the international state system in the twenty-first century as surely as the twentieth century swept away the colonial empires, and will usher in an era of harmony and peace; while many environmentalists, in contrast, fear that the industrial technological system is out of control and that it is almost too late to avoid irreversible damage to the ecological life-support systems of the planet, with the consequence that the world faces an era of environmental catastrophes and bitter conflicts over resources.

What is common to these pessimists and optimists, however, is the conviction that our fate is already settled by forces outside ourselves. For good or ill, we are in the grip of trends which we can do very little about. Some may rejoice at them, others despair, but there is doubt that we can any longer shape the future collectively, or that we should even try. For neo-liberals and for many postmodernists the future is about individuals and their choices. It is not about politics. Politics is generally disparaged as an activity, which is shrinking in importance and relevance.

Is politics at an end? This book has argued that it is not. The reasons are of two kinds. The first as laid out in the previous four chapters is that many of the claims about the end of history, the end of the nation-state, the end of authority and the end of the public domain are contestable; there are better ways of understanding the changes which we are living through, without resorting to hyperbole and fatalism. The second is to recognize that politics as an activity is not just part of our experience but constitutive of it. The fatalism implicit or explicit in so much of the writing on endism expresses particular political choices which not only exclude others, but suggest that no other choices are possible or viable.

The content and style of politics is constantly changing, and may be unrecognizable fifty years from now. But the need for politics will not disappear. Indeed, in this final chapter I want to argue that the need for politics has never been greater, because the scale of the problems facing us, which need collective action to be solved, has never been more daunting. If we cannot address these problems through politics, we cannot address them at all. The further implication of some of the writing on endism is that we do not need to address them, either because they are not problems or because they no longer require collective solutions. This is the most complacent view of all.

The Dimensions of the Political

Yet the political will not go away. The opening chapter examined its three dimensions – power, identity and order – and noted how politics has always been disparaged as an activity through its over-identification with the first of these dimensions – concerned as it is with affairs of state, the business of government, who's in and who's out, court politics and the twists and turns of policy. The fascination with power and influence, the love of in-fighting and political gossip, the petty and not so petty corruptions of office are endemic features of politics in any political system, and it is the trivial nature of much of it and the increasing exposure of it to public scrutiny in the media which gives rise to the low opinion in which politicians are often held. The lack of honesty in politics is exemplified by the common practice of politicians seeking to denigrate their opponents and misrepresent their views while at the same time equivocating and declining to state their own views openly. In many political systems voters have become cynical about politicians because they do not trust them to speak honestly; politicians are not believed because in public speech all their energy goes into making partisan points in the (increasingly vain) hope of embarrassing the other side, while in government many of their

actions are suspected of favouring the interests which
finance them or might finance them. The more professional politicians become, the more they come to
resemble a tribe set apart from the rest of society, with
their own peculiar rituals, beliefs and obsessive behaviour,
which the electorate observes and periodically is asked to
cast judgement on, as in some weird game show.

But this dimension of the political cannot be willed
away. Resources have to be allocated and positions filled
in any political system, and a politics will emerge around
them, to question and contest decisions, and to exert
pressure and influence. The issue is how extended or how
narrow the group making the decisions is to be. The
political class in any society can turn in on itself, no longer
open to the wider society, no longer involved in brokering
agreements between interests, or trying to build consensus. That would mark a change for the worse, but it would
not mean that there was no longer any politics. However
small the 'court' around the site of power, there will still
be a struggle to control that power, to determine its policy
and to speak on behalf of it. The smaller the court, the
more intense and incestuous the politics becomes.

This dimension of politics arises from centralized
decision-making. It is present in every organization, and
in contemporary states it is likely if anything to increase
since the appetite of the media for personalities and
political gossip shows no signs of abating; rather the
reverse. This is court politics and it has always existed; in
modern democracies it is rather more open and exposed
to view than it has ever been, which in turn has brought
pressure to impose constraints and limit abuses. In many
political systems, both democratic and authoritarian, corruption and clientelism are still rife. There are things that
can be done to make court politics less objectionable and
also less of an obstacle to getting policies through and

implemented, but court politics will always be a game of insiders and outsiders. It will always be noisy, and it will always be rough. It is not, however, the whole of politics, as some commentary suggests. But it is because it sometimes seems to be so that politics can appear as little more than froth on top of the deeper social trends determining our fate, like an orchestra playing frenetically on the upper deck of the *Titanic* as it ploughs on remorselessly towards the iceberg.

But to concentrate too much on politics as power neglects the other dimensions: politics as identity and politics as order. The values, principles, beliefs and commitments which define political identity distinguish friends from enemies, launch political movements and establish benchmarks and criteria by which we recognize political positions. This is connected with power in numerous ways but it is also separate from it, and it has a much more enduring quality than the careers of individual politicians and advisers. It is part of the background against which personal struggles are played out. For some political theorists the defining of friends and enemies is the essence of politics because it says who you are, what you stand for, and indicates a readiness to take action in defence of your interests and beliefs. Without friends and enemies, politics would have no point. Without conflict and serious disputes, the issue of who was in office and what their policies were would become trivial.

Many of the endism narratives either proclaim or imply that the sources of identity which are relevant for politics are disappearing in the modern world and that this is why politics is withering away. The narrative of the end of history with its proclamation that one of the great sources of political identity – ideological argument – is over, suggests that politics has no function any more. Similarly, the narrative of globalization purports to see an end to the nation-state and with it one of the most potent divisions to have influenced political identity. Ideology, however, is protean; it seems alive and well and still a potent source of identity and difference, and even if the nation-state were to disappear, of which there is little sign, there are other sources of difference which could fuel the politics of identity in the future. Ethnicity and gender, as well as many aspects of culture such as religion, remain key sources of identity. As political identity has become more complex, so the extent to which identity is constructed and negotiated rather than being imposed or inherited has increased.

The third dimension of politics, the politics of order, is concerned with how the political is constituted through the legal and political structures which provide the opportunities and constraints which shape political actions and outcomes. This dimension might seem more nebulous and less immediate than the dimensions of power and identity, but it is of the greatest importance, for it underpins politics as power, and its structures persist over long periods of time. This is the dimension of institutions, the rules which guide and shape behaviour, and embody norms and values. It includes different forms of governance, the ways in which societies are steered through certain key institutional modes, which include hierarchies (such as companies, government departments and agencies), markets (including financial markets, product markets and labour markets) and networks (such as policy and research communities and political movements).

This dimension includes constitutions, but not just the constitutions of states – the rules which determine such matters as voting, election, office-holding, terms of office, division of powers, centralization, devolution, powers, due process and individual rights – but also the constitutions of societies and economies, the rules and institutions which determine how these are governed and the ways they are sustained through formal and informal political processes.

Twisting Fate

If politics is confined in its meaning to the dimension of power, it is easy to see why it appears dwarfed by the vast impersonal forces which determine the fate of societies. But considered in the wider frame suggested here, politics is an activity which also creates and sustains forms of identity and forms of governance. It creates a political realm through which a community seeks control of its fate. But fate has different meanings. This book has argued that it is too often associated with vast impersonal forces, in the grip of which human beings become mere playthings of the gods. At one time these vast impersonal forces were identified with supranatural forces which controlled human destiny. Modernity promised to liberate human beings from the control of these supranatural forces and give them new capacities and powers, but modernity also unleashed secular forces which in time have fashioned a series of iron cages in which individuals and the whole human species are caught. The determinism of these strands of modern thought have spawned a fatalism, expressed very clearly in the writing on endism, which is dismissive of politics and its ability to make any difference.

If we wish to escape the fatalism which arises from modernity we have to embrace politics and contest the idea of inexorable trends grinding their way to inevitable results. But embracing politics does not mean discarding the notion of fate or thinking that human beings can make a sudden leap into a world free of constraints. The true relationship between politics and fate is an interaction between initiation, innovation and possibility on one side, and constraint, contingency and historical legacy on the other. This tension is central to our experience. Treating fate as a constraint on political action rather than as some unalterable destiny gives a different angle on the narratives of endism and how we should assess them. Three particular visions of our fate which endism promotes and which destroy the possibility of politics stand out and will be considered further here – the one-dimensional society, the global market and the technological state.

One-Dimensional Society

A one-dimensional society is a society in which there is no longer any way to construct, either in imagination or in practice, a viable alternative to the way in which society is organized. The triumph of liberalism means that free market capitalism and liberal democracy are all that there is, and they cannot be improved upon, although human societies can do worse if they choose. There is no longer any agency which might be the catalyst for revolution, nor any critical thought which can distinguish future possibility out of present circumstances.

This pessimistic reading of our times depends heavily on an identification of the only practical alternative to capitalism as the system of Soviet communism which came to a definitive end in 1991. But this is to freeze the meaning of capitalism and socialism in the particular historical opposition of two military, political and economic systems in the twentieth century. The clash of liberalism and socialism over the last century generated a powerful politics of identity around class and created political movements and a transformative politics of order which questioned the fundamental principles of social and economic governance.

Marxism had predicted that capitalism would be the last class mode of production known to history, and that a workers' revolution would bring about first a socialist and then a communist society. Control of the means of production would be vested for the first time in the hands of the producers themselves and the state would wither away. This dream of a solidaristic community which would utilize and develop the productive level which capitalism had established, and would be self-governing, redistributing resources according to need, proved incapable of realization in the circumstances of Russia, and its failure there eventually persuaded many of its former adherents that it could not succeed anywhere. Soviet Communism proved a cruel disappointment when it became first a dictatorship and then a tyranny, a state which put Soviet national interests ahead of world revolution, which caused the deaths of millions of its citizens through terror and which attempted to suppress any internal or external movements it could not control.

The subsequent revelation that the Soviet Union was economically backward and by the end completely unable to compete with the West completed the painful re-evaluation that had to be made not just of the Soviet experiment but of the entire Marxist project. The end of history was celebrated as it was because it was regarded as the end of Marxism. What the Russian experience shows, however, is not that alternatives to capitalism are unthinkable or impossible, but only that the particular opposition between socialism and capitalism which Marxism constructed failed to recognize the nature of the constraints inherent in modernity. These shortcomings were pointed out by Hayek and the Austrian school, but were long ignored. The core of their argument was that socialism

could not succeed in Russia or anywhere else because it
was at variance with the complexity of a modern economy
and modern society. The dream of solidarity, moral equality, sharing and community were pre-modern ideals,
unsuited to the qualities required for a society based on
individual property rights, interdependence, impersonality
and a specialized division of labour and market exchange.

The dreams of Marxism for a new society beyond
capitalism represented a retreat from complexity, and
therefore from modernity. The Bolsheviks had never
thought through the implications of governing a complex
modern economy, so that the command planning system
which they evolved meant in effect an attempt to impose
a simpler model of society, one in which the whole
economy was governed and co-ordinated from the centre
rather than through markets. They did not propose to go
back to self-sufficient agricultural communities, but
wanted to retain industry and continue the development
of modern technology. The result was a colossal failure.
Development was achieved at huge human cost and economic waste.

Soviet Communism might be cited as a typical example
of a failure of politics to thwart fate, an attempted rebel-
lion against the iron cage of modernity which had to admit
defeat. But the reason it failed was precisely its reckless
confidence in the power of political will to remake society
regardless of constraints, a confidence which was wholly
at variance with the precepts of Marx himself, who had
always leant in the other direction, stressing how much
agency was constrained by circumstances, and arguing
that new forms of society had always to evolve first within
the existing society, and could not be imposed prema-
turely through a political coup. The failure of the Soviet
Communist experiment does not then tell us that alternatives to the way in which modern society is organized are

impossible, but it does underline the importance of understanding that there are always constraints.

Two of the most important of these constraints for efficient economic organization in a complex, interdependent society are individual rights, including property rights, and decentralized markets. These core institutional features of the capitalist economy limit what politics can deliver. But that does not mean there are no alternatives within those limits. That would only be so if the unreal alternatives of capitalism and socialism as they were constructed in the nineteenth century continued to be accepted as the standard by which all others are judged. The possibilities for other alternatives to be determined and shaped through politics are extensive. There are many varieties of capitalism and different institutional arrangements, different legal systems, different roles for the state and different cultures. There is no single model, not even within a single national economy.

Politics has a key role in shaping forms of economic governance. The public domain becomes a key space for deliberation and determination of the public interest in relation to economic affairs between conservatives, neoliberals, socialists and social democrats, greens and many others. The debate is framed by core principles, particularly equality, efficiency, liberty and accountability, which raise major issues over how the governance of the economy should be constituted. The principles of the market order are anything but settled, and there remains a rich agenda to be explored and debated within socialism and liberalism. The idea that the discrediting of command planning finishes the argument about equality and how a society is best organized to allow all its citizens to participate fully in its life and develop their abilities to the utmost is particularly odd. Freed from the false utopia of a centrally planned economy which had abolished markets, money and the division of labour, left-of-centre thought is free to reinvent itself and reconnect with some of the better insights and ideas from its past, as well as the core values of modernity, including equality.

The notion that there are no longer any great ideological issues in the world is strange enough when applied to the countries where liberal capitalism rules supreme. But it becomes bizarre in relation to the vast populations which remain outside this magic circle, in Africa, in Asia, in Latin America and in the former territories of the Soviet Union. There, the big issues about economic and social development are still presented in a stark form, but there are few signs of progress towards resolving them. In several instances the obstacles to development have grown larger. During the twentieth century the hierarchy of rich and poor states hardly changed, testimony to the failure of capitalism so far to deliver its promise of universal development. The gap between the promise and the achievement of the western ideology will ensure that in the future new challenges to it will arise. The continued impoverishment of the South ensures that fundamental questions about distribution and economic and social organization will not go away.

The Global Market

In many narratives of modernity the global market is presented as one of its central tendencies. There have been setbacks and interruptions but if the history of capitalism has one clear outcome in these narratives it is the integration of all parts of the world into an interconnected economy. Globalization has been uneven, and many of these interconnections are much more extensive and have much greater depth in some regions than others.

A few areas have still barely been touched. But gradually over several centuries a global market has become a reality.

Alongside it from the beginning has developed a global civil society and a global polity, but more slowly. What many versions of the new discourse on globalization seek to do is to conflate all the tendencies towards globalization into a global market. It is presented as the manifestation of an inexorable social process which is heading in only one direction, and which demands that every country and every individual submits blindly to it as their fate. Politics and all its forms become redundant.

But no less than with the end of ideology these narratives express political choices, and are sustained by political means. The issue is whether the debate is to be closed down or opened up about the nature of this global market and its future development. Its future is a key question for politics in this new century. The global market does not exist outside politics, it is dependent upon politics and political choices.

The principal alternative to neo-liberal accounts of the development of the global market has in the past been Marxism. The Marxist narrative, shorn of its political illusions, provides distinctive insights into the evolution of global capitalism as a social and economic system which has been developing for several centuries and is only now beginning to achieve maturity and the development of its full powers. It is driven by competitive accumulation of capital, which explains both its dynamism and its unevenness. It develops through spurts and crises, in different regions and at different times. Blockages to development – political, cultural and economic – constantly emerge. Patterns of production become routinized and lose their competitive advantage; rigidities and inflexibilities emerge in particular markets and institutions. But all patterns of production and particular spatial deployment of resources and labour prove temporary. Sooner or later the dam bursts and capital in search of new opportunities to reproduce itself and to grow finds new opportunities. The old patterns are bypassed and eventually collapse because it is impossible to sustain them. States may attempt to do so for a time through subsidy, but eventually the subsidies have to be unwound. This process of creative destruction is the means by which new technologies, new forms of organization, new markets and new needs are brought into existence, and it has been the means by which the global market has been gradually constructed, as opportunities to expand spatially have been one of the chief means that capital has found to maintain and increase its profitability.

The Marxist narrative, however, no less than the neo-liberal narrative, has a fairly bleak message for human agency, since the role of politics seems to be purely reactive, either seeking to subsidize declining industries to delay the impact of competition on employment and past investments, or seeking to adjust the domestic economy to make it more compatible with the needs of global competition. In either case, all the dynamism, all the initiative comes from the process of capital accumulation itself, against which states increasingly appear powerless. They have only appeared powerful when the global market has fragmented, as in the era of protectionism and regional blocs after 1914. Local victories over capital when social democratic movements succeed in establishing welfare programmes, and employment protection and other social measures, are later threatened because in a different period of global competition they no longer seem affordable, but are so many costs which capital no longer wishes to bear and can seek to avoid by relocating production elsewhere. Domestic political pressure then rises for the state itself to overturn these arrangements in the interest of maintaining employment and profitability.

The undermining of social democratic regimes by the encouragement of a 'race to the bottom' in a period of intensified global competition is often alleged as evidence that the general tendency of the process of capital accumulation is not only uneven but involves increasing social polarization and social exclusion. A surplus population is created which cannot be absorbed into the high skill, high security sectors of the economy and is either left outside altogether or employed in low-wage service jobs. The contrast between wealth and poverty in the global market is starker today than ever, and the gap between different regions and countries as well as between different sectors and groups within countries appears to be both unbridgeable and increasing. These malign consequences are attributed to the consequences of competitive accumulation itself, but also in some accounts to the pursuit of the neo-liberal project for imposing free markets on the whole world regardless of the consequences. Neo-liberalism is seen as wedded to a programme which would obliterate all local and regional institutional differences in the interests of ensuring perfect markets. A single blueprint of western institutions is to be imposed on the whole world as the price of full membership of the global market. The cost of these experiments is high, as many countries have discovered. For Russia, the consequences have been particularly cruel. To be the subject of one western experiment in the twentieth century was bad enough. To be the subject of two seems a particularly malign fate.

Neo-liberalism is an ideological narrative which constructs the world in a particular way. It cannot construct it just in any way it pleases, and to the extent that it has a purchase on reality, it has an accurate understanding of some at least of the constraints which shape the global

market. It understands the supreme importance of profitability and the need to minimize costs on capital and
remove all obstacles to its working. In its disregard for the
social and political underpinnings of capital in civil society
and the state it expresses the capitalist ideal of being
totally mobile and free of all attachments. This reluctance
of capital to be embedded or tied down reflects a crucial
aspect of the way in which capitalism as an economic and
social system works. Critics are quite right to point out
that capital has to be embedded. The idea of a capital
accumulation that was somehow self-governing and could
dispense altogether with social and political institutional
support is a fantasy, even if one that is entertained quite
widely. But for any individual capital, it is not a fantasy.
Opportunities for free-riding, for displacing costs on to
others, will always be attractive. Neo-liberalism expresses
this logic in a stark form, by arguing that individual
capitals and nation-states have a strong incentive to
reduce their costs to a minimum so as to undercut
competitors.

What is mistaken is to suppose that globalization somehow imposes a neo-liberal policy as the only policy which
governments can adopt. That would be to accept that
nation-states and all other political agencies had been so
weakened by globalization that they were now completely
subordinated to its logic. What neo-liberalism in fact
represents is one political choice among several. One
version of neo-liberalism argues for neo-liberalism in one
country – using national sovereignty to make all domestic
institutions as compatible as possible with the demands of
globalization; another sees neo-liberalism as most effective
if it operates at the global level, incorporated in transnational institutions and agencies whose remit is to run the
global market according to neo-liberal principles free from
political interference. The first is the nationalist pro-

gramme of many right-wing parties which (as so often in the past) can also become protectionist under the slogan of 'fair trade'. If other states in the global market break the rules, the neo-liberal state has a right to retaliate. The second is the dream of central bankers and technocrats, who like currencies which are 'politician proof'. Neo-liberal nationalists are temperamentally isolationists; they believe strongly in the principle of national sovereignty and that states should remain self-governing. Any cooperation with other states has to be intergovernmental, and never supranational. Sovereignty cannot be pooled and it should not be given up.

There are other choices, for example the creation of regional blocs, whether based on civilizations or regional economic interest. What such blocs always require is a core state which establishes a sphere of influence within which it has jurisdiction and rights of intervention which are recognized by other blocs. The creation of regional blocs in the 1930s followed the breakdown of the international monetary arrangements and was a defensive reaction by states to protect employment and output in their own economies. The attempt by each leading state to ensure its control over territory and resources in its sphere of influence raised international tensions and became a cause of war, but at first there was an attempt to accommodate the expansionary aims of states. The argument that spheres of influence today should be based upon civilizations similarly suggests that world order should be based on a mutual understanding between the leading states of each civilization that they would not interfere in the internal affairs of a state belonging to another civilization.

Such stances accept a new fragmentation of the global market, and reject the argument that globalization has the capacity to create a new cosmopolitan world order which dissolves national antagonisms and bypasses nation-states. It sees the fledgling institutions for governing the global market as impositions by the dominant western powers which have no legitimacy and command no consent in the rest of the world. To make the world subject to a single set of norms and values can only be achieved by coercion, and if attempted would be violently resisted. Instead of a false universalism, world order should be based upon the recognition of difference and mutual respect and the incommensurability of different cultures and political systems.

This view certainly represents the return of politics, a new political ordering of the world, an attempt to re-impose political priorities and choices on the global market. But although it contains some important insights and provides a telling critique of some of the more naive assumptions of cosmopolitan order, it is also deeply flawed both in its analysis and its prescriptions. It creates a vibrant new politics of identity, new sets of friends and enemies, but it has no links to a transformative politics of order, and proposes no new ideas as to how the state, the economy and society are constituted, the principles, norms and rules which determine how it is governed and the frameworks within which individuals make choices. If the only political choice were the cosmopolitan order of the globalists and the self-contained civilizations of the culturalists, the future would be bleak.

But there are alternatives. Registering the importance of nation-states and regions need not mean that these have to be imagined in the isolationist terms which the free market nationalists or the culturalists suppose. There is currently interest in the notion of open regionalism, how regionalist projects can be developed which do not lead to closed blocs but to wider forms of engagement in the global market. An open regionalism is not exclusive. The construction of a currency union or a common market does not preclude participation, for example, in global discussions to increase trade cooperation through agencies such as the WTO. What an open regionalism creates is the possibility of improving the institutions through which the global market is governed and ensuring that political choices and arguments are brought to bear. At present, regionalism is very uneven in the global market, and is much better developed in Europe for example than in Africa. But the building of regional cooperation is an essential first step to creating forms of world order which are shaped by politics as well as by economics.

The scale of the problem needs emphasizing. The transnational forces pressing us towards a global market and global civil society are well advanced. But the construction of a transnational public domain and agencies with capacities to regulate and order these transnational developments are much less so. The inadequacies of the present organization of the WTO and the IMF and the World Bank have recently been exposed. To be fully effective, politics needs settled rule so that decisions are accepted as binding. One of the greatest challenges facing us is whether relevant forums and agencies which are genuinely inclusive can be developed to tackle the enormous disparities and unevenness within the global market, and the threats to the ecology of the earth. These are political problems; they will not be solved by any other means, and they dwarf most problems which have been faced in the past. In these circumstances the idea that politics is at an end seems a little premature.

The Technological State

A third vision of our contemporary fate conjured up by the writing on endism is the inexorable march of technology and the way in which it is outrunning our capacities to control it. H. G. Wells once called the modern age a race between education and catastrophe, although he could not have quite imagined how science itself would turn into one of the main engines of catastrophe. The sense of a runaway world whose complexity is expanding too quickly for human beings to develop new institutions to live with its consequences became very strong in the course of the twentieth century. Traditional authority of all kinds has been challenged by the rise of modern forms of authority, but now these in their turn are in danger of losing their legitimacy. The crisis of authority has spread to engulf not just traditional but modern forms of authority as well. Modernity is succeeded by postmodernity, in which there are no foundations, no objective standards, no fixed points, above all no universalism and no knowledge which is not constructed and relative.

In its pursuit of radical critique and deconstruction of the established truths of the modern era, postmodernism has performed a role similar to that performed by other varieties of radical critique in the past. But although radical critique is very effective at exposing assumptions and the logic of arguments, it is not sufficient in itself. It does not build a new framework of practical reason. If postmodernism remains at the level of critique, it can offer no guidance as to what should be done about all the modernist processes which are in full flow. The global market and the industrial-technological system are not fictions, but processes which shape the context of everyone's lives. It is not much consolation to be told that they are simply subjective constructions which have no more truth or authority than any other which we might entertain.

Postmodernism offers the ultimate grand narrative that there are no grand narratives. It mocks the pretensions of the doctrines of modernity to universalism, but is itself universalist in its denials that any form of knowledge can be considered authoritative. As a ground-clearing exercise this may have some value, but only if there is an attempt to develop a substantive practical politics to engage with the issues thrown up by modernity. The famous iron cages of modernity – science, bureaucracy and the global market – do not disappear simply because essentialist narratives are deconstructed. The technological state continues to dominate human affairs and to create problems which require resolution.

Within a postmodernist discourse various approaches have been mapped out. The first is to deny that anything in fact can or indeed should be done. It canvasses a retreat from politics, acceptance that the world is not only out of control but irreversibly so, and that political action or intervention is hopeless. Far better to concern yourself with your own affairs, and observe public events from a distance as a spectacle. Such deep fatalism about the contemporary human condition is now widespread. It represents a complete rejection of the public and the realm of the political, or any kind of public or collective commitments. Although it seeks to deny the fact, this is as much a political position as any other with its own very clear commitments.

A second approach seeks to deal with the problem of the weakening of faith in the authority of science and reason by resurrecting traditional sources of authority and seeking to breathe new life into them. These various species of fundamentalism reject the universalisms of modernity and celebrate values and doctrines which modernity was expected to bury. These provide anchors for many groups, and deep personal and political commitment to the movements and their campaigns, but they seem likely in most cases only to prosper in states which are at a low stage of development. Even here, coercion is generally required. In complex economies and societies these fundamentalisms appear incapable of attracting majority support, but even if they did they would not be capable of providing solutions without resorting to coercion.

The old certainties of modernist doctrines have gone for good, and the limits of universalism are much better understood now than before. But the need to find forms of authority which command legitimacy remains crucial in devising policy in complex societies. Many of the problems which science and technology have created through their industrial applications, as well as many of the problems of the global market, cannot be tackled except through the further development of our knowledge of both natural and social systems. There is no avoiding this dilemma, but if it is not to lead to the consolidation of a technological state which is unaccountable and the close ally of equally closed industrial and financial interests, the only solution is the development of new forms of politics. As with the other previous examples, leaving it to the dimension of power will not be sufficient. There also needs to be a transformative politics which creates new rules and new institutions as well as forging new identities which acknowledge for everyone the importance of science in their lives. What is required is a politics which can both confirm science as a key arbiter in resolving disputes about the public interest and at the same time insist upon new standards of accountability and openness by creating new institutions. A politics of the public interest which draws on the three dimensions of power, identity and order has to utilize certain forms of authority, but it also plays an important part in establishing them, creating the public space and the norms and procedures under which particular kinds of knowledge can be recognized as authoritative. This process can be tortuous and there can be many setbacks, but it remains an indispensable part of a democracy, and the need is for more of it not less. It is sometimes represented as government by technocrats and experts, and therefore as anti-democratic, and if it is separated from the democratic process then it can indeed become so. A politics of the public interest, however, has to find ways of making expertise legitimate in political terms. This means justifying it in terms of norms of impartiality, independence and accountability.

A Future for Politics

Compared to the problems faced by the planet and the human species, the capacities of politics seem woefully inadequate. There are deep structural obstacles to tackling the causes of inequality and poverty, and effecting even very modest redistribution of resources and opportunities. The development of the global market has outpaced the development of the institutional forms of governance. There is no point in seeking to stop the development of the global market. But there is every reason for trying to make sure that political development catches up with it. Preserving and extending the realm of the political, creating a transnational public domain, is a condition for any prospect of improving the way in which the global market is governed. It does not ensure it. But it creates the space in which it becomes possible. Whether it is realized depends upon the emergence of new forms of political participation, and the wide dissemination of information and knowledge.

One of the most important issues facing the world is transnational governance, whether ways can be found to enable cooperative solutions to emerge to the many problems facing the planet and the species, which means including all regions and peoples rather than defending rules which consolidate the power and interests of the states and interests which are already powerful. Governance has to be transnational if it is to be effective. There are many reasons for pessimism rather than optimism, but the arguments found in much of the endism literature are not among them.

Endism is a dead-end, both in its assumptions and in its conclusions. Far from politics coming to an end, the real struggles for an inclusive global democracy to match the global market are only just beginning. Far from equality being dead, it has never been more relevant to judging policies. The political choices are becoming fairly stark; we can choose isolationism and fundamentalism, or we can continue the wager with modernity, acknowledging the importance of democracy, science and capitalism in the creation of the modern world, recognizing their flaws as well as their benefits, and continuing the slow, painstaking work of building the kind of transnational polity which may ensure all of us a future. To act otherwise would be to surrender to a dismal fate.

Bibliography

Anderson, Perry, *A Zone of Engagement* (London: Verso 1992).

Anderson, Perry, *The Origins of PostModernity* (London: Verso 1998).

Arendt, Hannah, *The Human Condition* (Chicago: University Press 1958).

Arrighi, Giovanni, *The Long Twentieth Century* (London: Verso 1994).

Bauman, Zygmunt, *In Search of Politics* (Cambridge: Polity 1999).

Beck, Ulrich, *Risk Society* (London: Sage 1992).

Bell, Daniel, *The End of Ideology* (New York: Free Press 1960).

Berger, Peter and Luckmann, Thomas, *The Social Construction of Reality* (Harmondsworth: Penguin 1967).

Bobbio, Norberto, *Left and Right: The Significance of a Political Distinction* (Cambridge: Polity 1996).

Bohman, James and Rehg, William (eds), *Deliberative Democracy* (Cambridge: MIT 1997).

Castells, Manuel, *The Rise of the Network Society* (Oxford: Blackwell 1996).

Castells, Manuel, *The Power of Identity* (Oxford: Blackwell 1997).

Castells, Manuel, *End of Millennium* (Oxford: Blackwell 1998).

Cerny, Philip, *The Changing Architecture of Politics* (London: Sage 1990).

Coates, David, *Models of Capitalism: Growth and Stagnation in the Modern Era* (Cambridge: Polity 2000).

Cox, Robert, *Approaches to World Order* (Cambridge: CUP 1996).

Crick, Bernard, *In Defence of Politics* (Harmondsworth: Penguin 1964).

Dryzek, John, *Discursive Democracy: Politics, Policy and Political Science* (Cambridge: CUP 1990).

English, Richard and Kenny, Michael, *Rethinking British Decline* (London: Macmillan 2000).

Flathman, Richard, *The Public Interest* (New York: Wiley 1966).

Fukuyama, Francis, 'The End of History', *The National Interest* 16 (Summer 1989), 3–18.

Fukuyama, Francis, *The End of History and the Last Man* (London: Hamish Hamilton 1992).

Gamble, Andrew, *Hayek: The Iron Cage of Liberty* (Cambridge: Polity 1996).

Gamble, Andrew and Kelly, Gavin, 'The New Politics of Ownership', *New Left Review* 220 (November/December 1996), 62–97.

Gamble, Andrew and Payne, Anthony (eds), *Regionalism and World Order* (London: Macmillan 1996).

Gibbins, John and Reimer, Bo, *The Politics of PostModernity* (London: Sage 1999).

Giddens, Anthony, *The Consequences of Modernity* (Cambridge: Polity 1990).

Giddens, Anthony, *Beyond Left and Right* (Cambridge: Polity 1994).

Good, James and Velody, Irving, *The Politics of Postmodernity* (Cambridge: Cambridge University Press 1998).

Gray, John, *Enlightenment's Wake: Politics and Culture at the Close of the Modern Age* (London: Routledge 1995).

Gray, John, *False Dawn* (London: Granta 1998).

Hall, Stuart and Jacques, Martin (eds), *New Times: The Changing Face of Politics in the 1990s* (London: Lawrence and Wishart 1989).

Halliday, Fred, *Revolution and World Politics* (London: Macmillan 1999).

Held, David, *Democracy and the Global Order: From Modern State to Cosmopolitan Governance* (Cambridge: Polity 1995).

Held, David, McGrew, Anthony, Goldblatt, David and Perraton, Jonathan, *Global Transformations* (Cambridge: Polity 1999).

Hirschman, Albert, *The Rhetoric of Reaction* (Cambridge: Harvard University Press 1991).

Hirst, Paul, *Associative Democracy: New Forms of Economic and Social Governance* (Cambridge: Polity 1994).

Hirst, Paul and Thompson, Grahame, *Globalization in Question* (Cambridge: Polity 1996).

Hoogvelt, Ankie, *Globalization and the Postcolonial World: The New Political Economy of Development* (London: Macmillan 1997).

Huntington, Samuel, *The Clash of Civilizations and the Remaking of World Order* (New York: Simon and Schuster 1997).

Kumar, Krishan, *From Post-Industrial to Post-Modern Society: New Theories of the Contemporary World* (Oxford: Blackwell 1995).

Laclau, Ernesto and Mouffe, Chantal, *Hegemony and Socialist Strategy* (London: Verso 1985).

Laclau, Ernesto, *New Reflections on the Revolution of our Time* (London: Verso 1990).

Lash, Scott and Urry, John, *The End of Organized Capitalism* (Cambridge: Polity 1987).

Macintyre, Alasdair, *After Virtue: A Study in Moral Theory* (London: Duckworth 1985).

Marcuse, Herbert, *One Dimensional Man* (London: Routledge 1964).

Marquand, David, *The Unprincipled Society* (London: Cape 1988).

Marquand, David, *The New Reckoning: Capitalism, States and Citizens* (Cambridge: Polity 1997).

Mulgan, Geoff, *Politics in an Antipolitical Age* (Cambridge: Polity 1994).

Mulgan, Geoff (ed.), *Life After Politics: New Thinking for the Twenty-First Century* (London: Fontana 1997).

Oakeshott, Michael, *Rationalism in Politics* (London: Methuen 1962).

Ohmae, Kenichi, *The End of the Nation-State* (London: Harper Collins 1995).

Pierre, Jon (ed.), *Debating Governance: Authority, Steering and Democracy* (Oxford: OUP 2000).

Pierson, Christopher, *Hard Choices: The Politics of Social Democracy in the Twenty-First Century* (Cambridge: Polity 2000).

Putnam, Robert, *Making Democracy Work: Civic Traditions in Modern Italy* (Princeton: University Press 1993).

Rorty, Richard, *Contingency, Irony and Solidarity* (Cambridge: CUP 1989).

Ruggie, John, *Constructing the World Polity* (London: Routledge 1998).

Russell, Bertrand, *Political Ideals* (London: Allen and Unwin 1963).

Schedler, Andreas (ed.), *The End of Politics: Explorations into Modern Antipolitics* (London: Macmillan 1997).

Schmitt, Carl, *The Concept of the Political* (Chicago: University Press 1996).

Spengler, Oswald, *The Decline of the West* (London: Allen and Unwin 1932).

Turner, Bryan, *For Weber: Essays on the Sociology of Fate* (London: Sage 1996).

Walzer, Michael, *Spheres of Justice: A Defence of Pluralism and Equality* (Oxford: Blackwell 1983).

Weber, Max, 'Politics as a Vocation', in H. Gerth and C. Wright Mills (eds), *From Max Weber: Essays in Sociology* (London: Routledge 1948).

Williams, Roger, 'Technical Change: Political Options and Imperatives', *Government and Opposition* 28:2 (1993), 152–73.

Wolin, Sheldon, *Politics and Vision* (Boston: Little, Brown 1960).

Index

authority, 57–76, 116, 117

Bell, Daniel, 31, 36

capitalism, 13, 14, 30–3, 34,
  35, 39, 43, 69, 71,
  104–6, 107–9, 112, 120
communism, 26–7, 30–4, 38,
  53, 104–6
conservatives, 30, 34, 37, 57,
  59–69, 107

endism, 2, 5, 10, 12, 13, 14,
  16, 17, 23, 33, 77, 88,
  96–8, 101, 103–4, 116,
  120
Enlightenment, 13, 14, 20,
  29, 36, 54, 69
European Union, 44–5, 81

fatalism, 8, 12–14, 15, 17, 38,
  52, 54, 56, 57, 59, 77,
  88, 98, 103, 117
fate, 1, 3, 9–11, 15, 16, 38,
  56, 60, 65, 75, 94, 98,
  103, 106, 120
as contingency, 16–18
as destiny, 9, 11–13, 16
iron cages of, 14, 15, 49,
  70, 72, 103, 106, 117
neo-liberal conception of,
  90–1
Ford, 19
French Revolution, 27, 29, 30
Fukuyama, Francis, 19, 26,
  29, 33, 36
fundamentalism, 25, 65, 68,
  69, 117, 118, 120

GM food, 75
global market, 14, 40–2,
  45–6, 50–3, 55–6, 70,
  79, 96, 108–11, 116–17,
  119
globalization, 13, 38–56, 97,
  101–2, 108–9, 112–15
and hyperglobalists, 42–3,
  52, 79, 94, 97
and national sovereignty,
  10–14, 40–1
and regionalism, 44–5, 55,
  113–15

globalization (*cont'd*)
　and social democracy,
　　110–11
　and uneven development,
　　108, 111, 115
golden ages, 4, 56, 62–3, 70,
　71
governance, 8, 43–4, 46, 50,
　52, 56, 68, 80–3, 94,
　102, 103, 105, 107, 119,
　120
　multi-level, 81
　transnational, 43, 46, 52, 120

Hayek, Friedrich von, 105
Hegel, Georg Wilhelm
　Friedrich, 20, 27, 28, 29
history
　end of, 10, 11, 12, 14,
　　19–20, 26–31, 34, 36–7,
　　42, 101
　and historicism, 26–31

ideology, 20–3, 31–7, 45, 102

Kojeve, Alexandre, 27, 29

liberalism, 13, 19, 20, 21,
　24–7, 30, 34, 35–6, 48,
　54, 81, 104, 107

markets, 64, 67, 68, 79, 80,
　106, 107, 109, 111
Marx, Karl, 21, 27, 30, 78,
　106
Marxism, 30, 33, 47, 54, 81,
　91, 105–6, 109–10

media, 67, 72, 85–7, 96,
　99–100
　and public service
　　broadcasting, 86
modernity, 13–17, 20–2, 28,
　36–7, 66, 72, 74, 88,
　96–7, 103, 105, 108,
　116, 118, 120

neo-liberalism, 46–56, 66–7,
　78–9, 82, 89–91, 98,
　109, 111–12
　and public choice, 48–50,
　　89–91
new public management,
　78–9

Ottoman Empire, 10, 60

participation, 84, 87, 88, 107
pluralism, 54, 65, 68
　and relativism, 15, 21, 68
politics, 1–6, 15–18, 23,
　24–5, 34–5, 42, 43, 46,
　76, 77, 88–9, 93, 98,
　99–104, 109, 110,
　114–15, 117–20
　and anti-politics, 2, 4–5,
　　23, 51
　end of, 2, 9, 10, 12, 14, 34,
　　43, 55, 95
　identity, 4, 6, 7–8, 24–5,
　　61, 64–5, 101–2
　and media, 84–6
　order, 3–4, 6, 8, 102–3
　and personalities, 70, 85
　and the political, 2, 3–8,

24, 43, 52, 86, 88, 99, 100, 102, 117, 119
and postmodernism, 23–6
power, 5, 6–7, 8, 99–101
Popper, Karl, 26
postmodernity, 20–6, 66, 98, 116, 117
public domain, 3–4, 6, 67, 77, 83–4, 86, 87, 91, 93–5, 107, 115, 119
and accountability, 87–9
and civic engagement, 84–7
and end of government, 77–84
and public interest, 89–95
public intellectuals, 86
public interest, 1, 49–50, 77, 89–95, 107, 118–19

risk, 70–1

science, 13, 14, 58, 59, 61, 69, 72–6, 94, 97, 116–18, 120

socialism, 13, 14, 20, 21, 24, 30, 31–7, 47, 53, 104–7
sovereignty, 4, 40, 41, 45, 46, 51, 52, 55, 80, 113
Soviet Union, 31–3, 37, 39, 53, 62, 104–6, 108, 111
state, 4, 6, 7, 8, 11, 38, 40, 41, 47, 48–9, 50, 67, 73, 78–9, 80, 82–3, 91, 93, 94, 107, 110
international state system, 39–40, 42–3, 55, 97
welfare, 70, 78
sustainability, 73–4, 98

technology, 14, 75, 75–6, 88, 97, 116–19
tradition, 59–69, 70, 71

Weber, Max, 59
Westphalia, Treaty of, 39, 80
WTO, 82, 115

UN, 39